Python Networking 101

Second Edition

Mastering the capability of network and socket programming, AsyncIO, network performance, simulations and Ansible

Odette Windsor

Published by: GitforGits

Publisher: Sonal Dhandre

www.gitforgits.com

Printed in India

First Printing: November 2024

ISBN: 978-81-974165-0-7

Cover Design by: Kitten Publishing

Disclaimer:

This book, including all its text, diagrams, and illustrations, is an original work developed for educational and informational purposes. The content is not affiliated with, endorsed by, or sponsored by X, or any other company, brand, or entity referenced within. All brand names, product names, and trademarks mentioned are the property of their respective owners and are used in a descriptive, educational context only. Every effort has been made to ensure that no copyrighted or trademarked material has been copied or misused in this book. All diagrams and illustrations that are not original have been used with proper attribution and credit to their respective sources.

If we believe that any content in this book infringes upon the copyright or trademark, please contact us immediately at support@gitforgits.com. Upon notification, corrective action will be taken promptly.

Prologue

When I released the first edition of Python Networking 101, I honestly didn't expect it to get the kind of response it did from both Python programmers and networking professionals. We started out thinking we were building a practical, structured way to bring these two worlds together, and it turned out that many people who wanted to bridge the gap between coding and real network operations turned to it as their go-to reference. People liked that the steps were clear and easy to follow, with a focus on getting things done rather than on having a bunch of complicated theory. A lot of people wrote to me saying that it helped them automate tasks that they had been doing manually for years, while others shared how it gave them the confidence to switch careers or take on more advanced responsibilities in their roles.

Along with the praise came some really helpful feedback from the editor. As some readers pointed out, there was a need for more in-depth technical details in certain chapters, especially around asynchronous programming, SNMP operations, and network testing. Some suggested including more practical examples, ones that could run without much tweaking, while others asked for more seamless transitions between topics, aiming to create a more fluid learning experience. I took all of that seriously while putting together this second edition. We've reviewed, refined, and rebuilt every chapter to reflect current practices, tested libraries, and accurate workflows.

This second edition is for Python programmers who want to get into networking but don't want to feel overwhelmed. You'll start by getting a handle on the basics of Python and understanding the structures you'll use to build real network tools later on. Then, I'll walk you through the world of TCP, UDP, and socket programming so you can write working programs that communicate over networks. Then, you'll gradually explore application-layer protocols like HTTP, DNS, FTP, and email, and learn to interact with them programmatically. Once you've set up your base, the focus shifts to automation. I'll show you Netmiko, Paramiko, and NAPALM so you can control devices remotely and standardize configurations. You'll then move on to asynchronous programming using AsyncIO to handle network tasks efficiently. Then, I'll show you how to monitor, analyze, and test networks using SNMP, ping3, iperf3, Locust, and SimPy. You'll learn not just to gather information, but to act on it intelligently.

Another key thing for us is security. I'll show you how to set up firewalls, scan for vulnerabilities, encrypt data, and use VPNs to help you build safer network environments. In the later chapters, I talk about configuration management and orchestration using Ansible, so you can automate entire infrastructures and enforce consistency across servers and devices. This is a practical, structured journey that'll give you the real deal. Every concept is supported by working examples that you can try right away.

My goal is to make you comfortable with reading code and using it to solve real-world networking problems.

Content

Preface ..... *xii*

GitforGits ..... *xiii*

Acknowledgement ..... *xiv*

Chapter 1: Introduction to Python and Networking **1**

Chapter Overview *2*

Python Overview *2*

Setting up Python Environment *3*

Install Python 3.12 3
Create Virtual Environment 4
Install VS Code and Python Extensions 4
Install Core Libraries 4

Python Syntax and Data Structures *5*

Variables and Data Types 5
Operators and Strings 6
Conditionals, Loops, Functions and Arguments 6
Modules, Classes and Objects 6

Essentials of Networking *7*

Network Topologies 7
Networking Core Protocols 8
Routing, Switching, and Layered Models 8
Security 9
Modern Automation Tasks 9

Summary *10*

Chapter 2: TCP, UDP and Socket Programming **11**

Chapter Overview *12*

Transport Layer Protocols *12*

TCP (Transmission Control Protocol) 12
UDP (Transmission Control Protocol) 13
Choosing TCP vs UDP 13

Socket Programming in Python *14*

Types of Sockets 14
How Sockets Work? 14
Datagram (UDP) Sockets 15
Core Socket Functions 16

TCP Socket Programming 16
Creating TCP Server 17
Building Simple TCP Client 17
Sending and Receiving Data 18

Implementing a TCP Server and Client 19
Building TCP Server 19
Building TCP Client 20

UDP Socket Programming 20
UDP Server 21
UDP Client 21

Implementing a UDP Server and Client 22
Writing UDP Server 22
Building Flexible UDP Client 23

Summary 25

Chapter 3: Working with Application Layer 26

Chapter Overview 27

Application Layer Protocols Overview 27
HTTP and HTTPS 27
FTP 27
SMTP and IMAP 28
DNS 28

HTTP(s) Requests and Responses 28
How HTTP/HTTPS Works? 28
'requests' Library 29

Performing FTP Operations using 'ftplib' 30

Sending and Receiving Emails 32
Sending Emails with 'smtplib' 32
Receiving Emails with 'imaplib' 33
Coupling Email with Automation 33

Performing DNS Queries 34
DNS Queries using 'socket' 34
Advanced DNS Queries using 'dnspython' 35

Socket Troubleshooting 35
Common Socket Errors 35

Catching Errors ... 36
Timeouts and Non-blocking Operations ... 37

Summary ... *38*

Chapter 4: Exploring Network Automation ... 39

Chapter Overview ... *40*

Network Automation Concepts ... *40*

Netmiko and Paramiko ... *41*
Paramiko ... 41
Netmiko ... 42
When to Use? ... 43

Managing VLANs ... *43*

Executing Remote Commands ... *45*
Reading Inventory and Commands ... 45
Connecting, Running, and Saving Outputs ... 46
Automate Problem Identification ... 47
Parallelizing ... 47
Handling Unexpected Prompts ... 48

Retrieving & Modifying Device Configuration ... *48*
Automated Backup ... 48
Detecting Changes ... 49
Pushing Changes ... 49
Rollback ... 50

Updating Device Firmware ... *50*
Standard Workflow ... 50
Uploading Firmware ... 50
Setting Boot Variables ... 52

Summary ... *52*

Chapter 5: Network Monitoring and Analysis ... 53

Chapter Overview ... *54*

Understanding Network Monitoring & Analysis ... *54*
What Network Monitoring Really Means? ... 54
What About Network Analysis? ... 54

Exploring SNMP ... *55*
Key Concepts ... 55
SNMP Operations using PySNMP ... 56
SNMP GET (Grabbing a Single Stat) ... 56
SNMP WALK (Gathering a Whole Table) ... 57

SNMP SET (Changing Device State) 58
SNMP TRAP (Catching Alerts Instantly) 59

Network Traffic Monitoring *60*
Approach of Traffic Monitoring 60
Polling Device Counters 60
Sniffing Live Packets 61

Measuring Network Performance *62*
ICMP Ping 62
Advanced Testing using 'iperf3' 62

Analyzing Network Performance *63*
Analysis Approach 63
Analysis Workflow 63

Summary *64*

Chapter 6: Network Security and Python 65

Chapter Overview *66*

Setting up Firewall *66*

Scanning Network Vulnerability *67*

Secure Communication with SSL/TLS *68*

Exploring Scapy *69*

Establishing VPNs *70*
Automated Deployment of OpenVPN 70
Deploying WireGuard 72
Monitoring and Validating VPN Health 73

Summary *73*

Chapter 7: Working with APIs and Network Services 75

Chapter Overview *76*

APIs and Their Types *76*
APIs for Modern NetOps 76
Core API Concepts 76
Major Types of APIs 77
REST APIs 77
SOAP APIs 77
XML-RPC and JSON-RPC 77
Device-level APIs 78
GraphQL APIs 78

Working with APIs *78*

Using Python to Interact with APIs 79
Making a GET Request 79
Sending Data with POST and PUT 80
Handling Errors, Timeouts, and Rate Limits 80
Authenticating APIs 81
Pagination and Large Responses 81
Sessions, Retries, and Logging 82

Automatic Network Services 83

Summary 84

Chapter 8: Network Programming with AsyncIO 85

Chapter Overview 86

Introducing Asynchronous Programming 86
Need for Async 86
Synchronous vs. Asynchronous Workflows 86
Real Benefits for Network Engineers 87

AsyncIO Library 87
What Is AsyncIO? 87
Event Loops and Coroutines 88
Running Coroutines 88
Awaitables, Tasks, and Scheduling 89
Integrating AsyncIO 89

AsyncIO for IO Bound Operations 89
AsyncIO for IO-Bound 89
AsyncIO for Parallel API Requests 89
Handling IO-Bound Tasks 91
Async File Operations 91
Async Database Operations 91
Async Socket Operations 91
Error Handling and Throttling 91

Summary 92

Chapter 9: Network Testing and Simulation 94

Chapter Overview 95

Introduction to Network Testing and Simulation 95
Central to IT Services 95
What We Test, Measure, and Simulate? 95
Python Toolkit 96

Popular Network Testing Methodologies 97
Connectivity Testing 97

Latency and Jitter Measurement ... 97
Bandwidth and Throughput Testing ... 98
Load, Stress, and Soak Testing ... 98
Packet Loss and Error Rate Testing ... 98
Security, Vulnerability, and Compliance Testing ... 98
Simulation and Modeling ... 99

Performance Testing using ping3 and iperf3 ... 99
Measuring Latency and Packet Loss ... 99
Bandwidth and Throughput Testing ... 100

Reliability Testing using Locust ... 101
Exploring Locust ... 101
Configuring Locust ... 101
Demystifying Reliability Testing ... 102
Scripting Reliability Test ... 102
Analyze Reliability Test Results ... 103

Capacity Testing using Locust ... 103

Network Simulation with Simpy ... 104
Installing SimPy ... 104
Building a Simple Network Queue Simulation ... 104
Adding Parallel Simulation ... 106

Summary ... 106

Chapter 10: Network Configuration Management ... 107

Chapter Overview ... 108

Network Configuration Management (NCM) ... 108
Why NCM Matters? ... 108
NCM Core Objectives ... 108
Modern NCM Toolbox ... 109
Automating Configuration Management with Python ... 109

NAPALM for Version Control and Backup ... 111
Setting up NAPALM ... 111
Retrieving & Backing up Device Configurations ... 112
Accessing Device and Config ... 112
Retrieve Running Config ... 112
Save Config for Version Control ... 112
Comparing and Validating Configurations ... 113
Pushing and Rolling Back Configurations ... 113
Automating NAPALM for Scalability ... 114

Automating Configuration Restore Workflows ... 115
Working of Automated Restore Pipeline ... 115

Building Restore 116

Advanced Automation Orchestration *117*
Why Nornir? 117
Creating Device Inventory 117

Summary *119*

Chapter 11: Ansible and Python **120**

Chapter Overview *121*

Introduction to Ansible *121*
Control Node, Managed Nodes, and Inventories 121
Agentless Automation and Idempotence 121
Playbooks 122
Ansible and Python 122
Human-Centric and Scalable 122

Setting up Ansible on Windows *123*
Setting up WSL 123
Using Linux VM on Windows 123

Ansible Modules, Tasks and Playbooks *124*
Writing First Playbook 124
Making Playbooks Dynamic 125
Conditionals and Loops 126
Handlers 127
Includes and Roles 127
Error Handling and Idempotence 128
Writing Custom Modules 128
Sample Program: Pushing VLANs 129

Playbook to Configure Servers *130*
Defining Inventory and Groups 131
Writing Role-based Playbook 131
Variable Files and Template Management 133
Executing Playbook 134
Securing Sensitive Data 134

Ansible for Managing Softwares *135*
Package Management 135
Managing Post-Install Service State 136
Handling Software Upgrades 137
Working with Third-Party and Custom Software 137
Auditing and Enforcing Software Compliance 138
Sample Program: Enforcing Application Stack 139

Summary *140*

Index *141*
Epilogue *143*

Preface

If you're a developer getting into networking for the first time or an IT pro looking to build practical automation skills, this second edition gives you a clear and structured path to master essential networking concepts and become a confident, hands-on Python network administrator. If you're looking to automate repetitive networking tasks, build tools for infrastructure, or become a network administrator, you'll find this book teaching all the skills, structure, and mindset to make it happen.

You'll start off by getting the basics of Python down and then quickly move on to TCP, UDP, and socket programming. You'll work with protocols like HTTP, FTP, DNS, and email, and you'll use Python to automate everyday network tasks. As you read on, you'll dive into modern network automation using Netmiko, Paramiko, and NAPALM, manage asynchronous tasks with AsyncIO, and set up monitoring and analysis workflows through SNMP, ping3, iperf3, and Locust. You'll also use SimPy to simulate networks, program firewalls, scanning, encryption, and VPNs. You'll also get to work on configuration management and orchestration using Ansible. This will teach you how to automate server and network setups, manage software lifecycles, enforce standards, and integrate Python for advanced logic.

This book is all about clarity and practicality, using simple, easy-to-follow examples that work in the real world. It's not meant to deal with complicated business scenarios, but it does cover the most important, routine and common jobs of network programming.

In this book we will learn how to:

- Learn the basics of Python syntax and data structures for network automation.
- Get the hang of TCP, UDP, and socket programming for real communication tasks.
- Practice your skills with HTTP, FTP, DNS, and email protocols using real-world Python scripts.
- Set up SSH connections and device configurations using Netmiko, Paramiko, and NAPALM.
- Take charge of asynchronous network operations with Python's AsyncIO library.
- Keep an eye on, look at, and test networks using SNMP, ping3, iperf3, Locust, and SimPy.
- Make your network security stronger by using firewalls, scanning, SSL/TLS, and VPN configurations.
- Take advantage of the NAPALM and Git integration to automate your configuration management and version control.
- With Ansible playbooks, roles, and automation workflows, you can orchestrate server and network setups.

GitforGits

Prerequisites

If you're a programmer looking to expand your reach or a networking pro looking to automate, this book will give you the skills you need to feel confident. This book is perfect for self-learners, professionals, and career upgraders within Networking and System Administration.

Codes Usage

Are we in need of some helpful code examples to assist we in the programming and documentation? Look no further! Our book offers a wealth of supplemental material, including code examples and exercises.

Not only is this book here to aid we in getting the job done, but we have our permission to use the example code in the programs and documentation. However, please note that if we are reproducing a significant portion of the code, we do require us to contact us for permission.

But don't worry, using several chunks of code from this book in the program or answering a question by citing our book and quoting example code does not require permission. But if we do choose to give credit, an attribution typically includes the title, author, publisher, and ISBN. For example, "Python Networking 101 by Odette Windsor".

If we are unsure whether the intended use of the code examples falls under fair use or the permissions outlined above, please do not hesitate to reach out to us at support@gitforgits.com.

We are happy to assist and clarify any concerns.

Acknowledgement

I owe a tremendous debt of gratitude to GitforGits, for their unflagging enthusiasm and wise counsel throughout the entire process of writing this book. Their knowledge and careful editing helped make sure the piece was useful for people of all reading levels and comprehension skills. In addition, I'd like to thank everyone involved in the publishing process for their efforts in making this book a reality. Their efforts, from copyediting to advertising, made the project what it is today.

Finally, I'd like to express my gratitude to everyone who has shown me unconditional love and encouragement throughout my life. Their support was crucial to the completion of this book. I appreciate the help with this endeavour and the continued interest in my career.

CHAPTER 1: INTRODUCTION TO PYTHON AND NETWORKING

Chapter Overview

There's no doubt that Python's unique features make the language an essential tool for automating networking tasks of every size and scale. In this chapter, we will learn how to set up a modern, isolated Python environment on a Linux system. This way, every script we build is easy to maintain, share, and deploy.

Through hands-on exercises, we will learn the ins and outs of Python's variables, data types, functions, loops, and modules, just like network engineers do in their day-to-day work. There'll be a review of the basics of clean code, strong typing, and safe error handling, with a focus on patterns that help we prevent mistakes before they happen. And in this chapter, we will learn how to confidently organize automation scripts, manage dependencies, and use the same tools that pros use in real production networks. We will get a solid grasp on how core networking components, modern topologies, and the most-used protocols shape the tasks we will automate. As we go through it, we will see how network engineers, administrators, and security professionals use Python for everything from monitoring and compliance to troubleshooting and large-scale changes.

Python Overview

We all know how Python is widely recognized how this language changed the way network engineers, sysadmins, and automation architects work in the real world. The Python's first achievement in networking came when the community adopted it for writing scripts that controlled switches, routers, and servers, all thanks to its clear and readable syntax. Instead of hundreds of lines of shell or Perl, we can simply write small, focused Python scripts that do the same job, and they work everywhere, from a Linux jump box to a cloud VM. As Python matured, it didn't just stick with the basics. Over the last decade, its performance and error messages got a massive boost, especially with Python 3.11 and above. This matters when we troubleshoot live: the traceback tells us exactly where something broke, saving hours. We get async features that let us open hundreds or thousands of network connections in a single process with barely any extra code. That's made possible by a rock-solid standard library, improvements in packaging, and modern typing. Now, we run the same Python script on Ubuntu 22.04, Fedora 39, or even inside a Docker container, and the results are consistent, no strange bugs from OS quirks.

The network vendors started publishing their first-party SDKs in Python, not as an afterthought. We can control a Cisco switch, automate a Juniper firewall, or call an AWS networking API without leaving the Python ecosystem. For every networking task, we get a well-tested open-source library, such as we can use **`paramiko`** for SSH, **`netmiko`** for higher-level CLI access, **`napalm`** to normalize multi-vendor configs, and **`httpx`** for async HTTP APIs. If we want to work with SNMP, **`pysnmp`** is the tool. If we need to build or analyze network packets? One can use **`scapy`** or **`pyshark`** for serious power. These are not just toy libraries, rather most of these are used in production by Fortune 500s and cloud providers. We can find full telemetry integration with tools like **prometheus_client**, which means every automation we build can be monitored, traced, and debugged with industry best practices. The type annotations and static checking (**mypy**) allows us to safely refactor large scripts, and all the teammates see the same errors we do, before the code even runs. What makes Python stand out is how quickly we move from a proof-of-concept to a CI/CD-pipeline-ready automation. We write a network audit script, add a few tests with **pytest**, lint the code with **ruff**, and ship it in a container or straight onto a jump box. Every library we use is available from PyPI, and when we pin versions in **requirements.txt** or **pyproject.toml**, the project is reproducible by anyone, anywhere. All of this means when we join a new project or inherit a legacy environment, Python allows us onboard fast, build trust with automated checks, and expand the toolkit to cover everything from RESTful APIs to binary packet parsing. Over the next chapters, we will use real libraries, run actual commands, and build networking scripts that are tested and ready for production. I strongly keep a belief that the Python language isn't just for learning, it's for doing and innovating the world of software.

Setting up Python Environment

I'll show we how to set up the Linux machine as a solid foundation for Python automation. We'll open the terminal and make sure every step is crystal clear, tested, and verified. We recommend using Python 3.12, the latest version at this point, so we get the fastest code execution, best tracebacks, and maximum compatibility with modern libraries.

Install Python 3.12

If we are on Ubuntu 22.04 or similar, we need to add the Deadsnakes PPA for new Python builds:

```
sudo apt update && sudo apt install -y software-properties-
common
sudo add-apt-repository -y ppa:deadsnakes/ppa
sudo apt update
sudo apt install -y python3.12 python3.12-venv python3-pip
```

We can verify the same if it has been installed properly:

```
python3.12 --version
```

We should see something like this:

```
Python 3.12.2
```

If we don't get "Python 3.12.2" or later, stop here and paste the output, we'll fix it together.

Create Virtual Environment

For this, we first navigate to the project folder (let's use **~/networking101**), then:

```
python3.12 -m venv .venv
```

We then activate it:

```
source .venv/bin/activate
```

We will know it worked when the prompt starts with **(.venv)**. From here on, every Python and pip command runs in this safe space.

Install VS Code and Python Extensions

To get the editor, we then run:

```
sudo snap install --classic code
```

Now, we open the VS Code:

```
code .
```

In VS Code, we then install the official Python extension (search "Python" in Extensions panel and hit install). Once done, then press the **Ctrl+Shift+P**, and search for "Python: Select Interpreter," and pick the one from the **.venv** folder.

Install Core Libraries

Now here, we need a few essential libraries for network automation. So for this, we then type:

```
echo -e 'httpx\npytest\nruff\nmypy\nprometheus-client' >
requirements.txt
pip install -r requirements.txt
```

We then confirm with a real command and real output:

```
python -c "import sys, httpx; print(sys.version.split()[0],
httpx.__version__)"
```

We should see:

```
3.12.2 0.27.0
```

This output tells us we are running Python 3.12.2, and the latest **httpx 0.27.0**. If we get a different output, we can do debug versioning, pip issues, or dependency conflicts which I will teach we in later chapters.

After this, we then hit "Format on Save" within VS Code and check the bottom status bar for **(.venv)**. After this, then create a **.gitignore** with **.venv** in it, so the environment never gets committed by mistake.

And, for **ruff** and **mypy**, we need to add a **pyproject.toml**:

```
[tool.ruff]
line-length = 100
[tool.mypy]
python_version = "3.12"
strict = true
```

Now this we need to put into our root folder, and then we are well set for proper linting and type checking.

Python Syntax and Data Structures

We already know the basics of Python, but every solid project depends on using it well. This will help we know what we need to do to be successful. We want our syntax to have a clear purpose and our data structures to be chosen for dependability, speed, and clarity.

Variables and Data Types

One thing which everybodys knows about Python is that it doesn't require us to declare a type, but we still want to use variable names to tell the story. For instance, instead of **x** and **y**, we use **ip_address**, **interface_list**, or **device_status**. The main data types we will reach for are **int**, **float**, **bool**, **str**, **list**, **tuple**, **set**, and **dict**. The ability to use dynamic typing is a power, but we keep the code tight and safe by always knowing what type each variable should hold. So here, we can type the hints which will let us annotate:

```
def get_uptime(host: str) -> int:
    ...
```

So even in a dynamic language, we can build self-documenting and checkable code. If we are working with network gear, we might create lists of device names, sets of IPs to avoid duplicates, or dictionaries to map hostnames to config blobs.

Operators and Strings

We generally use **+**, **-**, *****, **/** for math, but Python's powerful operators also cover string concatenation, list appends, and membership checks. When we want to check if an IP address is in the list of blocked IPs, just write **`if ip in blacklist:`**. We can also rely on comparison (**==**, **!=**, **<**, **>**, **<=**, **>=**) and logical (**and**, **or**, **not**) operators every day in the scripts for access control and config checks.

Coming to the strings, most of the readable logging and device messages demand clear formatting. So here in python, the F-strings (**`f"Device {hostname} is up"`**) allow we interpolate variables directly. They're fast, safe, and make logs much more readable. We can always prefer f-strings for any text that goes into logs, alerts, or configs. So, for multi-line configuration templates, triple-quoted strings and **`.format()`** still have their place, but f-strings remain the default.

Conditionals, Loops, Functions and Arguments

In python, we generally make use of **if**, **elif**, and **else** to check statuses, decide actions, or gate changes. The loops (**for** and **while**) let us process device lists, interface counters, or batches of events. And, the list comprehensions (**`[dev for dev in devices if dev.status == 'up']`**) make for readable and efficient filtering. We can never nest loops too deep, break logic into small functions instead for clarity and easier testing.

We can also turn repeated logic into reusable, tested functions. We can use default arguments, keyword arguments, and type hints so the teammates always know what goes in and out. For automation, every function is a contract, inputs, outputs, and side effects are explicit. Also, the docstrings are not optional; even a one-liner makes life easier:

```
def is_valid_mac(mac: str) -> bool:
    """Returns True if string is a valid MAC address
format."""
    ...
```

Modules, Classes and Objects

In python, we can split the big scripts into modules, and that too one file per main topic or device type. In python, a package (**`src/netops/`**) allows us group helpers, parsers, and command runners. **`__init__.py`** signals a package, and relative imports keep code testable and portable. We can avoid circular imports by planning dependencies up front. If we or a teammate ever wonder where a function lives, we just follow the package path.

Now, for stateful or reusable behaviors, think of a session to a router or a device audit, so we can reach for a class. With **`__init__`**, we set up device state; with methods, we run actions. A

`Device` class might store hostname, IP, and connection state. We can use properties to keep attributes safe and private, and special methods like **`__str__`** or **`__repr__`** make debug logs readable.

The dataclasses are great for simple record-keeping, as shown in the below program:

```
from dataclasses import dataclass
@dataclass
class InterfaceStat:
    name: str
    rx_bytes: int
    tx_bytes: int
```

The above script keeps code clean, readable, and auto-generate equality checks.

After this, all the scripts and automations we write for networking tasks will be clear, reliable, and ready for anything, even a surprise device reboot or a broken API.

Essentials of Networking

All networks, from a small office to a huge data center, are like puzzle pieces that fit together in both the physical and virtual sense. First, we've got hardware: ***switches*** connect hosts in a LAN and segment broadcast domains using VLANs, while ***routers*** direct traffic between networks using static routes or dynamic routing protocols. They place ***firewalls*** in key spots to enforce security policies using access control and deep packet inspection. All the big enterprise networks use load balancers too. They're there to spread the application traffic around on the servers, so everything stays up and running smoothly. We can access the network wirelessly using standards like 802.11ac or 802.11ax for high-throughput Wi-Fi. We manage all of these with management stations, sometimes on physical servers, sometimes in VMs, and more often lately as containers or even serverless cloud functions. Things like cabling, patch panels, and transceivers are part of the physical setup, but these are also being tagged, inventoried, and mapped using automated discovery scripts these days.

Network Topologies

Generally, the shape of the network is designed based on business needs, growth plans, and resilience targets. In many small to medium environments, the ***star topology*** dominates, every device links to a central switch or router. It's simple, but if that hub fails, everything goes dark. So, to improve reliability, large enterprises and data centers adopt ***mesh*** or ***leaf-spine (Clos)*** architectures: multiple paths exist between every device pair, so losing a cable or a switch rarely means losing access. The ***Ring topologies*** can be seen in metro Ethernet, where traffic circulates for redundancy. In data centers, the ***fat-tree*** topologies scale bandwidth using uniform, layered switching, often automated with Zero Touch Provisioning (ZTP) and live topology mapping scripts. The cloud environments offer their own virtualized network overlays, using VXLAN, GRE, or even native SDN controllers that we control from Python SDKs and APIs. We must remember one thing, that every topology we work with influences how we automate device discovery, failover testing, or traffic engineering.

Networking Core Protocols

The function of networking is all about protocols, and those are nothing but the rules that let devices exchange data predictably, securely, and efficiently. At the lowest level, the ***Ethernet*** delivers frames within LANs; VLAN tagging (802.1Q) carves out logical networks for security or performance. Above that, there is ***IP (v4 and v6)*** gives unique addressing for every device, with routers forwarding packets according to static, dynamic, or policy-based routes. We can rely on ***ARP*** (for IPv4) or ***NDP*** (for IPv6) to translate IPs to MACs, filling device ARP tables that we will automate for troubleshooting or audits.

Now, when it comes to end-to-end connections, we depend on ***TCP*** for reliable, ordered, error-checked communication, ideal for critical control protocols, file transfers, and nearly all web traffic. The ***UDP*** offers low-latency delivery without guarantees, powering DNS, streaming, and telemetry. Modern applications increasingly use ***HTTP/HTTPS*** as their main language, every API, from cloud orchestration to network gear configuration, expects HTTP(S) requests. We need to script against these using libraries like **`httpx`**, always securing with TLS and checking certificates.

The ***DHCP*** hands out IP addresses and settings automatically, while ***DNS*** resolves hostnames to IPs; we will automate these to validate records, troubleshoot latency, or update dynamic inventories. The device monitoring, historically ruled by ***SNMP*** (polling and traps), is still everywhere, we automate interface stats, status polling, and alerting with Python's **`pysnmp`**. So, for CLI control, the ***SSH*** is the workhorse, no modern automation leaves home without Paramiko or Netmiko. The legacy networks might use Telnet, but we should always prefer SSH for encryption.

Routing, Switching, and Layered Models

We constantly interact with devices that run both switching and routing. The Layer 2 (switching) keeps traffic local, enforcing MAC learning and VLAN policies. The Layer 3 (routing) connects different networks using routing tables and protocols. In campus or branch networks, we will configure static routes for simplicity, or dynamic routing protocols, ***OSPF*** (link-state, fast convergence), ***BGP*** (scalable, Internet backbone standard), or ***EIGRP*** (Cisco proprietary, hybrid approach), for larger or more dynamic environments. The WANs use ***MPLS*** for fast, label-switched forwarding and traffic engineering; cloud and SD-WAN controllers abstract all of this, letting we manipulate policies with REST or gRPC APIs.

The ***OSI Model*** is the reference point, seven layers, from physical up to application. In automation, we need to focus most on layers 2-7: physical cables, data-link for MAC/VLAN, network for IP/routing, transport for TCP/UDP, session for sockets/connections, presentation for encoding, and application for protocols like HTTP, SNMP, SSH, or custom APIs.

Security

We know that the concept of security overlays everything. The network firewalls filter traffic based on policy, source, destination, port, protocol, and increasingly, packet content. The ***ACLs*** (Access Control Lists) are enforced on routers and switches to block unwanted flows at the source. For segmentation, we need to deploy ***VLANs*** and ***VRFs*** (virtual routing and forwarding), giving different departments or tenants isolated networks on shared hardware. The ***VPNs*** (site-to-site and remote access) encrypt data across public links, often using IPsec or SSL/TLS, and are managed by firewall or router appliances.

For data integrity, authentication, and privacy, one needs to enable ***802.1X*** on switches for identity-based port control. Increasingly, we also need to audit not just device configs but also flow logs (NetFlow, sFlow, IPFIX), intrusion detection/prevention (IDS/IPS), and event streams for real-time analysis. In fact, every automation script we write must respect security policies: always log changes, handle credentials safely, and use encrypted management channels. The python scripts integrate with secrets managers (HashiCorp Vault, AWS Secrets Manager) to pull credentials at runtime, not store them in code.

Modern Automation Tasks

In today's world, a network professional's daily routine is now built around automation. The concept of ***configuration management*** means not only pushing configs, but also taking regular backups, comparing changes, and validating against policy. With Python, we can audit thousands of devices for compliance, roll out firmware upgrades in safe windows, or bulk-update NTP, DNS, or SNMP settings across an entire fleet.

The ***network monitoring*** also has moved from manual polling to automated, event-driven models. We can easily set up scripts that gather interface stats, track link flaps, check health, and surface those metrics to dashboards (Prometheus, Grafana). The python's **`prometheus_client`** library allows us expose script metrics directly. When something breaks, we trigger auto-remediation routines, restart a stuck interface, reconfigure a lost VLAN, or send alerts to chat or ticketing tools.

Similarly, ***Inventory and topology mapping*** is also automated with SNMP, LLDP, CDP, and vendor APIs. The Python can build a live graph of the environment, visualize device relationships, and even document the network as it changes. We can automate access controls, generate and rotate credentials, or enforce password complexity rules across device fleets.

Today's networks aren't just cables and switches, they're software-defined and cloud-connected. We work with ***SDN*** (software-defined networking) controllers that centralize configuration,

EVPN/VXLAN overlays in data centers, and cloud-managed firewalls or routers. The ***Zero Trust Networking*** models are gaining ground, demanding identity-aware access at every hop, and we enforce this with microsegmentation and dynamic ACLs. In the cloud, we script against AWS VPCs, Azure VNets, or Google Cloud Networks using their Python SDKs, automating routing, peering, VPNs, and policy management. The ***network telemetry*** now streams in real time: gNMI, gRPC, NETCONF, RESTCONF, and OpenConfig expose structured, machine-readable device data, which we collect and analyze with Python clients. Machine learning is slowly entering the field for anomaly detection and predictive troubleshooting. The concept of ***wireless*** has grown beyond Wi-Fi, networks now manage BLE, Zigbee, LoRa, and even private 5G, and Python scripts talk to these through APIs, MQTT brokers, or direct device drivers.

In todays real-world, each networking specialist performs different automated roles, such as:

- ***Network Engineers*** architect, design, and troubleshoot both wired and wireless networks. They script configuration deployment, compliance audits, and topology visualization.
- ***Network Administrators*** run daily operations, onboarding devices, rolling out changes, responding to incidents. They automate monitoring, log analysis, and scheduled tasks.
- ***Network Specialists*** (data center, wireless, WAN, cloud) focus on tuning, scaling, or segmenting their domain, often automating failover, QOS, or provisioning.
- ***Security Professionals*** (SOC/NOC teams, auditors, architects) use Python to scan for vulnerabilities, parse and correlate logs, enforce policy, and even orchestrate incident response with playbooks.

As we move through this book, we will understand that every concept above will connect directly to code we write. When we automate config audits, we need to understand how protocols, topologies, and devices interact, otherwise scripts fail or cause outages.

Summary

In this chapter, we have learned why Python is the top choice for network automation. We learned to install and verify a modern Python environment, including working with virtual environments and integrating Visual Studio Code as a code editor. Then, we practiced using variables, core data types, operators, functions, string formatting, and robust error handling. We looked at how these choices affect reliability and clarity in automation projects.

Then, we explored the reasons behind choosing lists, dictionaries, sets, and classes to organize device information and state, and used type hints to increase code safety. We took a look at the usual Python patterns for logging, exception handling, and splitting code into modules and packages, and made them even better. We went over the basics of networking from both a practical and architectural perspective. This included how topologies, protocols, devices, and daily operational roles interact in modern networks. We chatted about real-world tasks and how automation can help with configuration management, monitoring, and security. We zeroed in on how all of this can be used in the real world.

CHAPTER 2: TCP, UDP AND SOCKET PROGRAMMING

Chapter Overview

In this chapter, we will take the first deep dive into the protocols and programming techniques that make real network communication possible. We will explore the differences between TCP and UDP, learning when to use each and how these protocols shape the way data moves across the internet and private networks. We will discover how to harness the socket library to build powerful, flexible network tools that can act as both servers and clients. Together, we will walk through the process of setting up TCP and UDP sockets, handling connections, sending and receiving data, and writing code that is robust in the face of errors or lost packets.

Next, we will then practice creating the own echo servers, simple messaging apps, and diagnostic tools, gaining hands-on experience that mirrors real production work. This will teach us to develop an intuition for troubleshooting, tuning, and extending socket-based scripts, making sure we understand not just the theory but the practical skills needed to build reliable and efficient network automation. The aim of this chapter is to make we confident to create apps that communicate over any network, such that we can be ready to learn the advanced networking topics ahead.

Transport Layer Protocols

We both know that most real networking work is built on a handful of protocols, and the two we will always run into first at the transport layer are ***TCP*** and ***UDP***. Both work at Layer 4 of the OSI model, but the way they handle connections, reliability, speed, and use cases couldn't be more different. When we automate, script, or troubleshoot any network application, whether that's a web server, a gaming backend, a monitoring probe, or a VoIP gateway, we are almost always working with either TCP or UDP under the hood.

TCP (Transmission Control Protocol)

Let's start with ***TCP***, the more heavyweight and "trustworthy" of the pair. We come to TCP whenever data integrity and order really matter. There are various use-cases like web browsing, email, file downloads, remote desktop sessions, or database sync jobs in which TCP contributes the best. The TCP sets up a connection between both endpoints, a three-way handshake that guarantees both sides are ready to talk. Once the connection is established, the TCP tracks every byte sent using sequence numbers and acknowledgment packets. If anything gets lost, out of order, or corrupted along the way, the TCP automatically detects this and retransmits the missing data, all without we having to write a single extra line of code for retries or reordering.

Another powerful thing this TCP does for us is flow control. For example, consider that we have a fast sender and a slow receiver. Here, the TCP automatically makes sure the sender never overwhelms the receiver's buffer, using a sliding window and smart algorithms to keep the stream balanced. On top of that, the TCP performs congestion control, adjusting the rate at which data is sent based on network conditions. If the internet or the internal network is getting bogged down, TCP scales back transmission rates, using mechanisms like slow start and congestion avoidance. Now, all of this happens transparently, so the applications can keep humming along even when network conditions fluctuate.

UDP (Transmission Control Protocol)

We now flip to the other side, which is the ***UDP***. The UDP is what we pick when speed, simplicity, and low overhead are more important than guaranteed delivery. The UDP is connectionless, which means it never bothers with handshakes or session setup. We just throw a datagram onto the network and hope it gets to the other side. If the packet is lost, corrupted, or duplicated, UDP simply doesn't care, and that's often by design. This protocol is best-suited for real-time applications like voice calls, online games, video streams, or monitoring sensors, where it's better to lose a packet occasionally than to pause and wait for retransmissions.

The UDP's biggest strengths are speed and efficiency. Because it skips reliability, ordering, and congestion control, UDP headers are much smaller, just 8 bytes compared to TCP's 20 bytes minimum. This reduces processing overhead and means data travels with lower latency. However, that also means the application must handle any reliability or sequencing logic itself if we need it. For many real-time systems, though, that tradeoff is perfect: missing a few voice samples or game state updates won't ruin the experience, but pausing for lost-packet recovery would.

Choosing TCP vs UDP

The best way to decide between TCP and UDP is to look at the application's needs. I recommend TCP if every byte of the data must arrive, in order, and only once, file transfers, web servers, databases, and secure remote logins all depend on it. On the other hand, we must choose UDP if we want speed, can tolerate some data loss, and need minimal overhead, like streaming, sensor feeds, or quick one-way notifications. Sometimes, we will see modern apps using both, in combination, and it is best suited for areas like streaming over UDP for real-time, and TCP for occasional, guaranteed control messages.

What makes this all real for we as a network automation pro is that we have full control over how the sockets and applications interact with both protocols. We can choose reliability, performance, or a mix, based on the requirements. We will see this in every network script, when we open a socket, set options, and decide whether the connection will be connection-oriented (TCP) or connectionless (UDP). When troubleshooting networks, being able to distinguish between TCP and UDP traffic helps we pinpoint why an application might be slow, unreliable, or even silent. If the monitoring probe using UDP misses an alert, we know to check for packet loss, not connection errors. If a TCP connection takes too long to establish, we will look for congestion, handshake problems, or firewall rules. These protocols are at the heart of every device, every tool, and every Python network script we write. In practice, both the TCP and UDP underpin almost everything we automate, test, or debug.

Socket Programming in Python

Once we are familiar with TCP and UDP, the real magic of automation and networking happens when we put those protocols to use in code. The ***Sockets*** are the Swiss Army knife for network programmers. Every network communication in Python, whether it's web scraping, device automation, data collection, or even running the own services, starts with creating and managing sockets. For example, just think of a ***socket*** as the endpoint of a two-way communication channel between devices, one end on the machine, one on the remote. Each socket is defined by an IP address and a port number. When we want two programs to talk over a network, they both open sockets and agree on which protocol (TCP or UDP) and which port to use. This pairing lets the script or server "listen" for connections, "dial out" to another machine, send or receive data, or even run bi-directional services.

So here, we start with first importing the **socket** library:

```
import socket
```

Types of Sockets

There are two main types of sockets in practice, ***stream sockets*** (for TCP) and ***datagram sockets*** (for UDP). The stream sockets (**SOCK_STREAM**) establish a connection and keep it alive for reliable, ordered, and error-checked data transfer. And, the datagram sockets (**SOCK_DGRAM**) just throw packets onto the network, with no guarantee they'll arrive or in what order. The choice or the selection among them depends entirely on whether we want reliability (TCP) or raw speed (UDP).

So, for stream (TCP) sockets:

```
tcp_socket = socket.socket(socket.AF_INET, socket.SOCK_STREAM)
```

And, for datagram (UDP) sockets:

```
udp_socket = socket.socket(socket.AF_INET, socket.SOCK_DGRAM)
```

Both of them make use of **AF_INET** for IPv4 addressing.

How Sockets Work?

A typical ***server*** creates a socket, binds it to an address (IP and port), and listens for connections. The following script shows how the server creates the socket:

```
server_socket = socket.socket(socket.AF_INET,
socket.SOCK_STREAM)
```

```
server_socket.bind(('127.0.0.1', 12345))
server_socket.listen(5)
```

Here, the server waits for up to five clients to connect. Each incoming connection is handled with:

```
client_socket, client_address = server_socket.accept()
```

The client, meanwhile, just creates a socket and connects:

```
client_socket = socket.socket(socket.AF_INET,
socket.SOCK_STREAM)
client_socket.connect(('127.0.0.1', 12345))
```

Once connected, we send and receive data:

```
client_socket.send(b"Hello, Server!")
response = client_socket.recv(1024)
```

The server receives and replies:

```
data = client_socket.recv(1024)
client_socket.send(b"Hello, Client!")
```

Now while we do all these, we must remember to close sockets when done. Doing this will free the resources:

```
client_socket.close()
server_socket.close()
```

Datagram (UDP) Sockets

The UDP sockets are even simpler because we don't need to "connect", just send and receive:

```
server_socket = socket.socket(socket.AF_INET,
socket.SOCK_DGRAM)
server_socket.bind(('127.0.0.1', 12345))
data, client_address = server_socket.recvfrom(1024)
server_socket.sendto(b"Hello, Client!", client_address)
```

So for this, on the client:

```
client_socket = socket.socket(socket.AF_INET,
socket.SOCK_DGRAM)
client_socket.sendto(b"Hello, Server!", ('127.0.0.1', 12345))
response, server = client_socket.recvfrom(1024)
```

In this, no handshake and no connection state, it is just the packets that are flying back and forth. If anything is lost, our app needs to deal with it. Another thing is that the python sockets are very highly configurable. It allows us to set timeouts, tune buffer sizes, or tweak options with **`setsockopt()`**.

Core Socket Functions

The thing that makes **`socket`** so essential is the way it wraps all the messy, low-level networking details into simple, Pythonic calls. With just a few lines, we can create servers, build clients, control connections, and send or receive any kind of data, raw or structured, across the network. The library is highly cross-platform such that the code we write on Linux laptop will run the same way on Windows or macOS. The scripts are extremely portable right out of the box.

Following are the ***core socket functions*** we will actually use every day:

- **`socket.socket()`** creates a new socket object.
- **`.bind()`** attaches the socket to a specific IP address and port, this is how servers "listen" for connections.
- **`.connect()`** is what clients use to reach out to a server.
- **`.listen()`** turns the bound socket into one that's ready to accept incoming TCP connections.
- **`.accept()`** returns a new socket object for each connected client and their address.
- **`.send()`** and **`.recv()`** are the bread and butter for moving data over TCP.
- **`.sendto()`** and **`.recvfrom()`** are used for UDP, where each message goes to or comes from a specific address.
- **`.close()`** always releases the resources when done.

It's worth remembering: ***everything in higher-level Python networking, HTTP clients, SSH libraries, SMTP, FTP, even most async frameworks, is built on top of this socket library.*** If we master these calls, we are set for almost anything in the field. Each example we write will make the underlying behavior clearer, so when we eventually hit performance or reliability snags, we will know exactly where to look and what to tweak. From here, let's jump right into TCP socket programming and make those abstract concepts concrete.

TCP Socket Programming

The TCP's main strength is its guarantee that if we send data, it gets there, in order, or we will know something's wrong. This is why everything from web servers to file transfers, email, and even some real-time messaging tools still rely on TCP.

Creating TCP Server

We now begin with the server side. So here, we will create a script that waits for clients to connect and sends them a greeting. For this, we create the following script:

```
import socket
server = socket.socket(socket.AF_INET, socket.SOCK_STREAM)
server.bind(('127.0.0.1', 9001))
server.listen(5)
print("Listening on port 9001...")
while True:
    client, addr = server.accept()
    print(f"Connection from {addr}")
    client.send(b"Hello, TCP Client!\n")
    client.close()
```

In the above script,

- The server socket is created and bound to **localhost** on port **9001**.
- **.listen(5)** sets up the socket to queue up to five incoming connections.
- The infinite loop calls **.accept()**, which blocks until a client connects.
- Once a connection comes in, we send a greeting, print the address, and close the client socket.

We can run this script, then in another terminal, connect with **telnet 127.0.0.1 9001**, and see the greeting printed.

Building Simple TCP Client

Now we move on to switch the roles. The client script is even simpler than the server one as shown below:

```
import socket
client = socket.socket(socket.AF_INET, socket.SOCK_STREAM)
client.connect(('127.0.0.1', 9001))
```

```
msg = client.recv(1024)
print("Received:", msg.decode())
client.close()
```

The client connects to the server at **localhost:9001**, waits for a message, prints it, and then exits.

Both these scripts give us an instant feel for TCP's handshake and stream-based operation. We never have to worry about missing or out-of-order packets, since the TCP's guarantees take care of that.

Sending and Receiving Data

After this, we want to send and receive more than one message per connection, and maybe handle different clients at once. So here, the TCP sockets can block (wait for data), so we will often use timeouts, non-blocking mode, or select/poll to manage multiple connections efficiently.

So accordingly, we can make a quick improvement to our server to echo back whatever the client sends with the following script:

```
import socket
server = socket.socket(socket.AF_INET, socket.SOCK_STREAM)
server.bind(('127.0.0.1', 9002))
server.listen(5)
print("Echo server on port 9002...")
while True:
    client, addr = server.accept()
    print(f"Client connected: {addr}")
    data = client.recv(1024)
    while data:
        client.sendall(b"Echo: " + data)
        data = client.recv(1024)
    client.close()
```

After this, we can now connect with **telnet 127.0.0.1 9002**, type lines of text, and see them echoed back with an "Echo:" prefix.

In the next topics, we will see how to scale this up, handle concurrent clients, and build services that are fast, resilient, and ready for anything.

Implementing a TCP Server and Client

In this topic, we will now actually build a working TCP server and client. Let us consider that we want to allow multiple users connect to the server and get a live status message or a custom service. So for this, we will write a script that will start the server, then the client, and then will ensure they work together.

Building TCP Server

We will create a simple "echo server" that listens on a local port, accepts client connections, and sends back anything it receives. For this, we will create a file called **`tcp_server.py`** and write the following script:

```
import socket
def run_tcp_server(host='127.0.0.1', port=8888):
    server = socket.socket(socket.AF_INET, socket.SOCK_STREAM)
    server.bind((host, port))
    server.listen(5)
    print(f"Listening on {host}:{port}")
    while True:
        client, addr = server.accept()
        print(f"Connection from {addr}")
        data = client.recv(1024)
        while data:
            print(f"Received: {data.decode().strip()}")
            client.sendall(b"Echo: " + data)
            data = client.recv(1024)
        client.close()
        print("Client disconnected.")
if __name__ == "__main__":
    run_tcp_server()
```

This will wait for clients, echo back everything they send, and print messages about each interaction. We can also connect to it from another terminal with **telnet 127.0.0.1 8888** or from any TCP client.

Building TCP Client

Now, we make another file called **tcp_client.py**. This client connects, sends a message, receives the reply, and then closes the connection:

```
import socket
def run_tcp_client(host='127.0.0.1', port=8888,
message="Hello, Server!"):
    client = socket.socket(socket.AF_INET, socket.SOCK_STREAM)
    client.connect((host, port))
    print(f"Connected to {host}:{port}")
    client.sendall(message.encode())
    data = client.recv(1024)
    print(f"Received from server: {data.decode().strip()}")
    client.close()
if __name__ == "__main__":
    run_tcp_client()
```

In this, we first start the server, and then we run the client. After we run the script, we will see the server echo the message and both scripts will print what's happening in real time.

Basically, at start, the server attaches to an IP and port, making it available to clients. Every time a client connects, the server gets a new socket object just for that client. Now, both sides can send and receive in both directions as long as the connection stays open. The data comes in as bytes, so we use **.decode()** and **.encode()** to work with strings. This structure is behind every chat app, monitoring service, REST API, and even parts of tools like Ansible or custom CLI-based automation we will build later.

UDP Socket Programming

Now we will get into what happens when we drop the guarantees and go for speed. The UDP is a different animal, there's no connection, no handshake, and no guarantee that the message will arrive. But it's lightweight, fast, and ideal for when we can tolerate some data loss, like in real-time monitoring, games, voice, or sensor data.

UDP Server

So here, we first create a file called **udp_server.py** in the similar manner we did in the previous TCP implementation:

```
import socket
def run_udp_server(host='127.0.0.1', port=9000):
    server = socket.socket(socket.AF_INET, socket.SOCK_DGRAM)
    server.bind((host, port))
    print(f"UDP server listening on {host}:{port}")
    while True:
        data, addr = server.recvfrom(1024)
        print(f"Received from {addr}:
{data.decode().strip()}")
        reply = f"ACK: {data.decode().strip()}"
        server.sendto(reply.encode(), addr)
if __name__ == "__main__":
    run_udp_server()
```

Now here, we don't have to call **.listen()** or **.accept()**. The server just waits for packets and replies to whoever sends them.

UDP Client

Now, we make the **udp_client.py** as shown below:

```
import socket
def run_udp_client(host='127.0.0.1', port=9000,
message="Hello, UDP Server!"):
    client = socket.socket(socket.AF_INET, socket.SOCK_DGRAM)
    client.sendto(message.encode(), (host, port))
    print(f"Sent: {message}")
    data, addr = client.recvfrom(1024)
    print(f"Received from server: {data.decode().strip()}")
if __name__ == "__main__":
```

```
    run_udp_client()
```

Once we start the server and run the client script, it will send a message, and the server will print what it got and reply with an "ACK". Now here, I have observed some of the most important points:

- The clients and servers don't "pair up", they just send and receive.
- Each packet is independent, so we can send or receive in any order.
- If we send ten packets, they might arrive out of order, or some might never show up.

As we go deeper, we will start to see why some automation tools use TCP for reliability, and others pick UDP for speed, now we know exactly how both work, and how to script each in Python.

Implementing a UDP Server and Client

There's no handshake or connection setup with UDP. Each packet is self-contained. The server is on a known port, just waiting for packets to come in. The client, anywhere on the network, sends a message to that port. If the server is up, it'll get the packet and be able to reply. If not, the message just disappears, and we don't get any errors or feedback. There's a lot of freedom with UDP, but we have got to be prepared to handle loss and uncertainty on the own.

Writing UDP Server

We first begin with writing a UDP server that's more than just "Hello World." It'll listen on all network interfaces, handle multiple incoming clients, respond to each sender, and include robust error handling.

Following is a real-world UDP server script:

```
import socket
import time
def run_udp_server(host='0.0.0.0', port=9001):
    server = socket.socket(socket.AF_INET, socket.SOCK_DGRAM)
    server.bind((host, port))
    print(f"[{time.strftime('%H:%M:%S')}] UDP server running
on {host}:{port}")
    try:
        while True:
            try:
```

```
                data, client_addr = server.recvfrom(4096)
                message = 
data.decode(errors='replace').strip()
                print(f"[{time.strftime('%H:%M:%S')}] Received 
from {client_addr}: {message}")
                timestamp = time.strftime('%Y-%m-%d %H:%M:%S')
                reply = f"Server {timestamp}: got '{message}'"
                sent = server.sendto(reply.encode(), 
client_addr)
                print(f"[{time.strftime('%H:%M:%S')}] Replied 
to {client_addr}, {sent} bytes sent")
            except Exception as e:
                print(f"[{time.strftime('%H:%M:%S')}] Error: 
{e}")
    except KeyboardInterrupt:
        print(f"\n[{time.strftime('%H:%M:%S')}] Server 
shutting down gracefully.")
    finally:
        server.close()
if __name__ == "__main__":
    run_udp_server()
```

In the above script,

- We first bind to **'0.0.0.0'**, due to which, the server listens on all interfaces, so clients can be local or remote (subject to firewalls).
- The **recvfrom(4096)** is non-blocking until a packet arrives. The buffer is set to 4KB, plenty for most UDP uses.
- Every packet is logged with a timestamp and sender's address, essential for debugging in real operations.
- The replies always go to the sender's IP and port. Since UDP is stateless, we don't have to "track" clients.
- The **finally** block ensures the socket always closes, preventing "Address already in use" errors on restart.

Building Flexible UDP Client

We now write a client that sends multiple messages, waits for replies, and demonstrates how the timeouts help we avoid waiting forever if something goes wrong.

```
import socket
import time
def run_udp_client(server_host='127.0.0.1', server_port=9001,
repeat=3):
    client = socket.socket(socket.AF_INET, socket.SOCK_DGRAM)
    client.settimeout(1.5)  # Wait at most 1.5 seconds for a
reply
    for i in range(repeat):
        message = f"UDP packet {i+1} at
{time.strftime('%H:%M:%S')}"
        try:
            sent = client.sendto(message.encode(),
(server_host, server_port))
            print(f"[{time.strftime('%H:%M:%S')}] Sent {sent}
bytes: {message}")
            data, addr = client.recvfrom(4096)
            reply = data.decode(errors='replace').strip()
            print(f"[{time.strftime('%H:%M:%S')}] Received
reply from {addr}: {reply}")
        except socket.timeout:
            print(f"[{time.strftime('%H:%M:%S')}] No response
(timeout waiting for server).")
        except Exception as e:
            print(f"[{time.strftime('%H:%M:%S')}] Error: {e}")
        time.sleep(1)  # brief pause between sends
    client.close()
    print(f"[{time.strftime('%H:%M:%S')}] Client closed
socket.")
if __name__ == "__main__":
```

```
    run_udp_client()
```

In the above client script,

- Each message is tagged with the current time, useful when we want to trace packets or debug network lag.
- **`settimeout(1.5)`** is critical: the client will not hang forever. If the network drops a packet or the server is slow, we will know.
- We send three packets, one per second. Adjust **`repeat`** to test with more or fewer.
- Each reply prints the sender's address, which allows us spot if replies are spoofed, NAT'ed, or relayed.
- Every error is caught and logged, so we never wonder why a test "just stopped working."

We can try changing the port, running from another machine, or shutting down the server mid-test to see timeout handling in action. On a local network, we will see how fast UDP can be. Across the internet, or with a flaky Wi-Fi, we will notice how some replies may never return.

With these UDP scripts, we got to see every granular step needed to build, test, and extend stateless network tools. We can debug, log, and recover from errors, all essential skills for any automation engineer.

Summary

Throughout this chapter, us took the understanding of transport layer protocols and put it to work, learning exactly how TCP and UDP power network communication in the real world. We practiced choosing the right protocol for the job, balancing the need for reliability with the speed and efficiency of datagram transmission. We got our hands on the Python socket library, exploring how it gives us all the building blocks needed for both client and server programming. We wrote scripts from scratch to create TCP servers and clients, mastering how connections are established, managed, and safely closed after data exchange. We then built UDP servers and clients, gaining a true feel for stateless, fast, and lightweight message passing.

Every step included robust error handling, timeouts, and techniques for handling multiple clients or network events. We learned how to debug, extend, and test the code under real conditions, making the network tools as reliable as those used in production environments. By the end of this chapter, we gained the skills and confidence to build, analyze, and automate TCP and UDP communications, setting yourself up for even more advanced networking tasks in Python.

CHAPTER 3: WORKING WITH APPLICATION LAYER

Chapter Overview

This chapter's going to teach we how to automate all the networking stuff that makes those apps run smoothly. We will start by understanding the role of application layer protocols, and we will discover why HTTP, HTTPS, FTP, DNS, and email are critical to nearly every workflow we automate. We will get to use Python to send and receive web requests, handle files across FTP servers, and manage emails as both notifications and automation triggers. This chapter's got we covered on how to do both basic and advanced DNS queries. That means the scripts can find, validate, and adapt to changing endpoints.

As we move forward, we will practice handling network errors with confidence, learning how to diagnose, log, and respond to real-world failures in the scripts. We will see practical patterns for handling and fixing errors that'll make the automation reliable, easy to maintain, and ready for production. By the time we are done with this chapter, we will have a handy, practical toolkit for building, integrating, and troubleshooting all the application-layer workflows we will come across in network engineering and automation.

Application Layer Protocols Overview

When we look at how modern networks power the world, from web browsing and video calls to email, cloud storage, and even IoT, the application layer is where it all gets real for users and automation engineers alike. This is the layer where humans and machines interact directly with the network, using protocols designed to solve actual problems: sharing web pages, sending files, exchanging emails, and translating human-friendly names to IP addresses. Every time we visit a website, check the email, upload a file, or even type a URL, we are depending on an application layer protocol. We can think of these as the "languages" applications speak on top of the underlying transport and internet layers. Without them, we would have raw packets but nothing meaningful happening, no data moving between apps, no content being delivered, and no services actually working.

The following ones are some of the most common yet powerful protocols:

HTTP and HTTPS

Both are the backbones of the web. Every browser, API client, automation tool, and web server talks in HTTP, requesting and serving up resources with simple, human-readable methods like GET, POST, PUT, and DELETE. HTTPS takes everything good about HTTP and adds encryption and authenticity, letting we shop, bank, and share private data securely. The Python scripts can work with both using libraries like **`requests`** for client tasks or **`http.server`** and frameworks for server-side logic.

FTP

The FTP is the go-to for moving files between servers and clients. It's used in legacy automation, backup routines, firmware updates, and even bootstrapping new systems. Despite being an older protocol, it's still everywhere, and we can interact with it natively in Python using the built-in **ftplib**.

SMTP and IMAP

The SMTP moves email from client to server and between servers. IMAP allows us read, organize, and manage email on the server, which is crucial for modern email apps and multi-device sync. We will script with **smtplib** and **imaplib** to automate alerts, manage mailboxes, or pull notifications into dashboards.

DNS

And, finally the DNS which translates the domain names humans use into the IP addresses computers need. Every time we script a network scan, health check, or web scraper, the code relies on DNS lookups behind the scenes. The Python's **socket** library handles this, but there are also specialized DNS modules for more advanced queries and diagnostics.

What ties all these protocols together is their focus on interoperability and extensibility. For example, an automated monitoring system might use HTTP to pull metrics, SMTP to send alerts, and DNS to verify endpoints, all inside a single workflow. The scripts will often move seamlessly between protocols, reading config from an FTP site, querying HTTP APIs, and sending results over email. In the chapters ahead, we will get hands-on with each of these, learning not just what they do, but how to use them in the real world, testing, automating, and integrating them into the own networking projects.

HTTP(s) Requests and Responses

Let me give you one big fact and that is every time we automate web tasks, hit a REST API, or test a cloud service, we are speaking HTTP or HTTPS. We will use it for everything from simple downloads and uploads to authentication, form submission, and real-time data exchange.

How HTTP/HTTPS Works?

The HTTP is a request-response protocol. The client (your browser, Python script, or monitoring tool) makes a request to a server. The server processes the request and sends back a response, maybe an HTML page, a JSON blob, or even just a status code. The HTTPS is the same protocol, but all data in transit is encrypted using TLS (or SSL), so eavesdroppers can't read or tamper with the requests or responses. This is mandatory for anything sensitive, logins, payments, personal data, or automation that interacts with secure APIs.

Both these protocols ride on top of TCP, HTTP on port 80, HTTPS on port 443 by default, but the magic is in how they package, transmit, and interpret data.

'requests' Library

Most of the automation projects will have us acting as a client, fetching data, posting updates, or triggering actions on remote servers. The python's **requests** library is the weapon of choice. It makes HTTP as easy as calling a function and handling the result.

- Install Requests

```
pip install requests
```

- Making a GET Request

A GET request retrieves information. We will use this for downloads, API reads, or status checks.

```
import requests
response = requests.get('https://www.example.com')
print(response.text)
```

The response object gives us everything: the raw content, HTTP status code, headers, and, if we call **response.json()**, any JSON-formatted data returned by the API.

- Making a POST Request

A POST request sends data to the server, maybe to authenticate, submit a form, or upload a file.

```
import requests
data = {'username': 'kitten', 'password': 'mypass'}
response = requests.post('https://www.example.com/login', data=data)
print(response.text)
```

The POST can carry form data, files, or even raw JSON.

- Handling Status Codes and Errors

Here, we will use **raise_for_status()** to catch any non-200 replies:

```
response = requests.get('https://www.example.com')
try:
    response.raise_for_status()
except requests.exceptions.HTTPError as e:
    print(f"Request failed: {e}")
```

This makes the scripts more robust, critical for automation that needs to alert or retry on errors.

- Working with JSON APIs

Most of the modern APIs use JSON. Parse it instantly:

```
response = requests.get('https://api.example.com/data')
if response.ok:
    data = response.json()
    print(data)
```

- Adding Headers

The APIs often require headers, API keys, tokens, custom user agents:

```
headers = {'Authorization': 'Bearer YOUR_TOKEN', 'User-Agent':
'my-python-script'}
response = requests.get('https://api.example.com/secure',
headers=headers)
```

Having these tools at the disposal gives us the green light to build scrapers, monitoring checks, API clients, automation scripts, and even test harnesses. We will be writing scripts that log into services, submit forms, download and parse data, or chain requests together to automate business logic. With HTTPS, everything is private and tamper-proof by default.

Performing FTP Operations using 'ftplib'

This is another classic protocol we will use in many automation tasks. The ***FTP (File Transfer Protocol)*** is everywhere for moving files between servers, routers, backup systems, and legacy devices, even if it's older, it's not going away anytime soon. We will find FTP in use for network firmware updates, bulk log transfers, nightly backups, and data ingestion between business systems. While HTTP(S) is best for APIs and web content, FTP shines whenever we need to push or pull large files, automate firmware or config uploads to network gear, or grab datasets from legacy business partners. Even modern cloud and hybrid infrastructures sometimes bridge old and new using FTP. That's why it's important for our scripts to speak this language fluently.

The python's built-in **`ftplib`** module gives us a simple, reliable way to connect to FTP servers, authenticate, list directories, upload, download, and delete files. The best part is that we don't need to install anything extra, just import and go.

- Connecting and Authenticating

We will generally start by creating an FTP object and logging in:

```
from ftplib import FTP
ftp = FTP('ftp.example.com')
ftp.login(user='youruser', passwd='yourpass')
print("Connected and logged in to FTP server.")
```

If we don't pass credentials, most servers allow us to connect as 'anonymous', but for anything important, always use real credentials.

- Listing Files and Directories

After this, to see what's on the server, we then use:

```
ftp.retrlines('LIST')
```

We can also navigate directories with:

```
ftp.cwd('/target-directory')
```

- Downloading Files

We then pull files from the server with:

```
with open('local_copy.txt', 'wb') as f:
    ftp.retrbinary('RETR server_file.txt', f.write)
print("File downloaded successfully.")
```

- Uploading Files

We can push files up with:

```
with open('upload.txt', 'rb') as f:
    ftp.storbinary('STOR upload.txt', f)
print("File uploaded successfully.")
```

After all this is done, never forget to close the connection:

```
ftp.quit()
```

There are many automation tasks that involve picking up config backups, pushing firmware images, or syncing log files with remote systems. In python, we can loop over many files, apply logic to skip or filter, and wrap all actions with error handling. Once we are automating file movement, we will often need to notify someone, maybe to alert on a successful upload, send a log summary, or distribute backup reports. That's where automating email with Python becomes the next skill.

Sending and Receiving Emails

The email remains a cornerstone of automation, delivering alerts, reports, system notifications, and more, right where we need them. In network operations, we might use email to notify about completed jobs, critical device failures, daily summaries, or compliance results. Again here, the python gives us powerful tools to both send and receive emails as part of any automated workflow.

Sending Emails with 'smtplib'

The python's built-in **smtplib** makes sending emails straightforward. The module talks to SMTP servers, just like the email client, and supports plain text, HTML, and attachments.

Let us consider a sample program of sending a notification as below:

```
import smtplib
from email.message import EmailMessage
msg = EmailMessage()
msg['Subject'] = 'Automation Complete'
msg['From'] = 'me@mydomain.com'
msg['To'] = 'admin@yourdomain.com'
msg.set_content('The nightly backup script finished
successfully.')
with smtplib.SMTP('smtp.yourdomain.com', 587) as smtp:
    smtp.starttls()  # Upgrade to secure connection
    smtp.login('me@mydomain.com', 'mypassword')
    smtp.send_message(msg)
print("Email sent!")
```

the above script then logs in, builds a simple text message, and sends it securely. We can extend it for multiple recipients, add CC/BCC, or send HTML by using **msg.set_content()** with HTML.

In addition, if we want add attachments like to send log files, configs, or reports:

```
with open('report.txt', 'rb') as f:
```

```
    msg.add_attachment(f.read(), maintype='application',
subtype='octet-stream', filename='report.txt')
```

Receiving Emails with 'imaplib'

The receiving and parsing emails is useful for automating responses to inbound alerts, approvals, or monitoring requests. The python's **imaplib** handles this job.

Following is a simple program of connecting and fetching emails:

```
import imaplib
import email
mail = imaplib.IMAP4_SSL('imap.yourdomain.com')
mail.login('me@mydomain.com', 'mypassword')
mail.select('inbox')
typ, data = mail.search(None, 'ALL')  # We can filter, e.g.,
'UNSEEN'
for num in data[0].split():
    typ, msg_data = mail.fetch(num, '(RFC822)')
    msg = email.message_from_bytes(msg_data[0][1])
    print(f"From: {msg['From']}, Subject: {msg['Subject']}")
    # If we want the body:
    if msg.is_multipart():
        for part in msg.walk():
            if part.get_content_type() == 'text/plain':
                print("Body:",
part.get_payload(decode=True).decode())
    else:
        print("Body:", msg.get_payload(decode=True).decode())
```

This above script logs in, reads the inbox, fetches each email, and prints details. We can also filter for unread messages, look for certain subjects, or parse attachments.

Coupling Email with Automation

Once the scripts can send and receive emails, we can close the loop: every automated task, backup,

FTP transfer, config change, or device audit, can trigger a clear, timely notification. We can even build auto-responders, escalate critical issues, or feed messages into ticketing or chat systems. If the organization uses OAuth2 or app passwords for email, then there are python libraries like **oauthlib** or specialized modules to simplify.

Next, we'll extend these communication skills into our next topic on DNS queries and real troubleshooting.

Performing DNS Queries

Very oftern, we may run into the need to translate human-friendly domain names into IP addresses, and this is where the DNS (Domain Name System) comes into play. Every automated script that interacts with web APIs, downloads files, sends alerts, or scans network devices depends on DNS, even if we don't see it working in the background. The DNS is the "phone book" of the internet. Without it, we would have to remember every device or service by its IP address.

The automation of the DNS queries helps to:

- Validate target systems before running scripts or tests.
- Resolve service records for complex setups (load balancing, failover, SRV records).
- Check if a domain has changed its IP (important for security or migration).
- Perform reverse lookups (IP to hostname) to improve logging or auditing.

DNS Queries using 'socket'

For the basics, we can use the standard **socket** library to resolve hostnames to IPs and vice versa as following:

- Forward Lookup (Domain to IP)

```
import socket
hostname = 'www.python.org'
ip_address = socket.gethostbyname(hostname)
print(f"{hostname} resolves to {ip_address}")
```

- Reverse Lookup (IP to Hostname)

```
ip = '138.197.63.241'
host = socket.gethostbyaddr(ip)
print(f"{ip} resolves to {host[0]}")
```

Now these simple tools are handy for most automation, but sometimes we will need more, like querying MX (mail) records, TXT records, or even SRV records used by advanced services.

Advanced DNS Queries using 'dnspython'

To get more control, we can make use of the python's **dnspython** package. It makes easy to perform any type of DNS query, such as for example to query different record types as shown below:

```
pip install dnspython
import dns.resolver
result = dns.resolver.resolve('python.org', 'A')
for ipval in result:
    print('A record:', ipval.to_text())
mx_records = dns.resolver.resolve('python.org', 'MX')
for mx in mx_records:
    print('MX record:', mx.to_text())
txt_records = dns.resolver.resolve('python.org', 'TXT')
for txt in txt_records:
    print('TXT record:', txt.to_text())
```

We might use DNS queries to check if a service has failed over to a backup IP, confirm that an API endpoint is reachable, or even validate that certain records exist before we proceed with configuration pushes. The DNS lookups often become part of monitoring, troubleshooting, and compliance checks.

Socket Troubleshooting

It's not always easy to predict what will happen in the world of network automation. Sometimes the connection fails, DNS doesn't resolve, firewalls block traffic, or a remote host drops we with no warning. It's all about learning to handle these errors, and recover or alert when they happen. That's what makes the scripts go from being "demos" to real, production-ready tools. We'll break this down into small, easy-to-follow steps, each focusing on a specific type of failure that we will likely encounter.

Common Socket Errors

Every network script will hit some combination of the following errors over time:

- Timeouts

The server or remote host didn't reply in time. Maybe the network is slow, the server is busy, or something dropped the packet. In Python, this triggers **socket.timeout**.

- DNS Failures

The hostname can't be resolved. The domain may be wrong, DNS is down, or we are on a network with no external access. The Python raises **socket.gaierror** (get address info error).

- Connection Refused or Reset

The target IP is reachable, but the port is closed, the service isn't running, or a firewall dropped the SYN. We will see **ConnectionRefusedError** or **ConnectionResetError**.

- Broken Pipe / Network Unreachable

Midway through data exchange, the connection drops, maybe a device rebooted, or the route changed. The Python gives **BrokenPipeError**, **OSError: Network is unreachable**, or similar.

- Address Already in Use

Your script tries to bind to a port that's already taken. It happens if we don't close sockets properly, or another process uses that port.

Each of these has a root cause and a best-practice for how to recover or log it in automation.

Catching Errors

Now here, a well-structured socket script will function appropriately. It can trap all known errors, logs what happened, cleans up, and either retries or exits cleanly.

Following is a sample program:

```
import socket
import time
try:
    sock = socket.socket(socket.AF_INET, socket.SOCK_STREAM)
    sock.settimeout(4)
    sock.connect(('93.184.216.34', 80))  # example.com IP
    request = b"GET / HTTP/1.1\r\nHost: example.com\r\n\r\n"
    sock.sendall(request)
    response = sock.recv(4096)
```

```
    print("Response:", response.decode(errors='replace'))
except socket.timeout:
    print("[ERROR] Timeout: No response from server after 4
seconds.")
except socket.gaierror:
    print("[ERROR] DNS lookup failed. Check the hostname or
network.")
except ConnectionRefusedError:
    print("[ERROR] Connection refused. The port may be closed,
or a firewall is blocking you.")
except ConnectionResetError:
    print("[ERROR] Connection reset. The server closed the
connection unexpectedly.")
except BrokenPipeError:
    print("[ERROR] Broken pipe. Data couldn't be sent, likely
due to a dropped connection.")
except OSError as e:
    print(f"[ERROR] General OS error: {e}")
except Exception as e:
    print(f"[ERROR] Unexpected problem: {e}")
finally:
    try:
        sock.close()
    except Exception:
        pass
```

Now, in the above program, we:

- trap each type of error individually to give clear, actionable logs or alerts.
- the **finally** block ensures the socket always closes, even if the script fails midway.

The use of **errors='replace'** in **decode()**, ensures the script never crashes on odd binary or mixed data.

Timeouts and Non-blocking Operations

The timeouts ensure the script doesn't hang forever, and it is very essential in any automation pipeline. Now, we can set the timeouts on both socket creation (**`settimeout()`**) and any blocking calls like **`connect()`** or **`recv()`** as shown in the following code:

```
sock.settimeout(2)  # Wait at most 2 seconds for any operation
```

Now there are some field proven troubleshooting tips which I have collated for us to use. They are:

- We need to test the script against unreachable IPs, closed ports, or DNS failures to see real errors.
- If a server crashes, restart the script and watch for "Address already in use", this means cleanup is needed.
- For UDP, just beware of silent drops. We need to always implement timeouts, and never assume we will always get a reply.
- The Ethernet need to be unpluged, kill Wi-Fi, or to use firewall rules to force errors and validate the handling.

It's really important to learn how to spot, catch, and fix socket errors, because that's what makes the code ready to be used in the real world. Every error is an opportunity to make the automation stronger, easier to troubleshoot, and safer to run at scale.

Summary

Throughout this chapter, we explored the major protocols and services that define the application layer in networking. We learned how HTTP and HTTPS requests work, sending and receiving web data securely with Python scripts, and handling everything from simple downloads to advanced API automation. We practiced moving files with FTP, connecting to remote servers, uploading, and downloading content, and then tied those workflows directly into automated notification by sending emails using Python's SMTP libraries. We discovered how to receive, read, and process emails programmatically for true end-to-end automation. We then worked through DNS queries, both simple hostname lookups and advanced record checks, to make the scripts resilient and dynamic in real-world conditions.

Finally, we focused on robust error handling and practical troubleshooting, covering everything from DNS failures to timeouts and resource cleanup. Each topic built on the last, helps us to connect, transfer, notify, and recover from problems across a variety of protocols. By the end of this chapter, we had gained the skills to automate, integrate, and troubleshoot every core application protocol used in modern networks.

Chapter 4: Exploring Network Automation

Chapter Overview

In this chapter, we'll go over automating the essential tasks that network engineers deal with every week. This includes discovering and configuring devices, upgrading firmware, and detecting drift. We will see why automation is important, not just for saving time, but also for making the network more reliable, secure, and auditable. We'll be using Netmiko and Paramiko as our main automation tools to connect, configure, and monitor devices from different vendors. We will get to practice building routines for VLAN management, running commands at scale, and backing up configurations with just a few lines of Python.

As we move forward, we will learn to handle complex scenarios like parallel connections, prompt handling, error recovery, and safe firmware upgrades. By the time we are done with this chapter, we will know exactly how to create the own automation toolkit. With it, we will be able to control the network safely and efficiently, and we will always know what we are doing.

Network Automation Concepts

When we first hear "network automation," we might think it's all about scripting away simple tasks. But in reality, it's a foundational shift in how networks are managed, operated, and secured at every scale, from a few routers to entire global backbones. The modern automation allows us move from manual, device-by-device management to orchestrated, policy-driven, and repeatable workflows that save massive time, prevent human error, and unlock agility across the network.

We've all been there with the hassle of logging into each device, typing out commands, checking status, and hunting for typos. When we are dealing with hundreds or thousands of devices, mistakes are bound to happen. With automation, we can make changes across all devices in seconds, check the status of the network with one script, and always roll back safely if something goes wrong. There's more to automation than just speed. It's also about making the network more reliable, more predictable, and easier to secure and audit.

Following are the key elements of network automation:

- Device Discovery

The automation starts with knowing what's on the network. Scripts using tools like Nmap or SNMP walk the infrastructure, build inventories, and spot rogue or misconfigured gear in real time.

- Configuration Management

The standardizing and maintaining the device configs is critical. The automation pushes golden configs, tracks every change, and can even validate compliance with internal policies or industry standards. We need to integrate with Git for version control so we always know who changed what, when, and why.

- Change Deployment and Rollback

With automation, we can push a new policy or firmware everywhere at once, but more importantly, we can roll back instantly if a change causes problems. This minimizes downtime and makes big upgrades much less stressful.

- Monitoring and Alerting

The automated monitoring pulls real-time health, performance, and security data. We can trigger alerts or even self-healing scripts when certain thresholds or anomalies are detected.

- Reporting and Auditing

The scripts generate up-to-date reports on network status, device inventories, compliance gaps, and more, giving we visibility for audits, capacity planning, or incident response.

Let's say we are setting up a new branch office. When we use automation, we just plug in a few IPs, run the scripts, and the whole switch stack is discovered, configured, secured, and ready to use in minutes. When we are trying to figure out what's going on, we can automate some basic checks, check the status of the interface, the routing tables, the logs, and get diagnostics from all the devices at once. The python is a key part of almost every major network automation framework. With python, it's a breeze to read, a snap to write, and has a huge ecosystem of libraries built specifically for networking (Netmiko, Paramiko, NAPALM, pyATS, and many more). It allows us glue together APIs, device CLIs, data models, and monitoring tools, so we can build custom solutions for any network, any vendor, and any requirement.

Netmiko and Paramiko

In the world of network automation, the ***Paramiko*** and ***Netmiko*** are two of the most important Python libraries, each with a unique role, but often used together to unlock full automation power.

Paramiko

The ***Paramiko*** is meant for raw SSH and SFTP automation. It allows us programmatically log in to almost any SSH-enabled device, run commands, and transfer files securely. It is a pure Python implementation of the SSHv2 protocol, so it works anywhere Python does, no extra dependencies, and no need for **`expect`** or shell hacks.

Following are the key features:

- It supports password, public key, and even multi-factor authentication.
- We can run any command on the remote shell and capture stdout/stderr for parsing or alerts.
- It securely transfers files, like configs, logs, or firmware images, to and from the devices.
- We can build our own SSH-based tools, daemons, or tunnels for unique automation needs.

To quickly install, we need to simply run:

```
pip install paramiko
```

Following is a sample program wherin we are running the command via SSH:

```
import paramiko
client = paramiko.SSHClient()
client.set_missing_host_key_policy(paramiko.AutoAddPolicy())
client.connect('192.168.56.101', username='admin',
password='mypass')
stdin, stdout, stderr = client.exec_command('show version')
print(stdout.read().decode())
client.close()
```

This opens a secure session, runs the command, captures the output, and closes the connection. We can loop this for dozens or hundreds of devices, parse output, or upload files via SFTP as part of the workflow.

Netmiko

While Paramiko gives us low-level control, the ***Netmiko*** takes the automation even to the next level through its:

- Multi-vendor Support
- Simplified Connections
- Command Abstraction
- Robust Error Handling

Now, to install it, just simply run:

```
pip install netmiko
```

We can try the following program that shows interfacing on a cisco device:

```
from netmiko import ConnectHandler
device = {
    'device_type': 'cisco_ios',
    'ip': '192.168.56.101',
    'username': 'admin',
```

```
    'password': 'mypass'
}
conn = ConnectHandler(**device)
output = conn.send_command('show interfaces')
print(output)
conn.disconnect()
```

The Netmiko is built on Paramiko but adds smarter handling for prompts, config modes, and device quirks. With just a few lines, we can automate configuration backups, mass changes, VLAN management, or real-time diagnostics across hundreds of devices, no vendor lock-in.

When to Use?

The most suitable application of ***Paramiko*** is when we want low-level, raw SSH or SFTP, need to automate Linux servers, or build fully custom SSH tools. Similarly, we can use the ***Netmiko*** for multi-vendor networking, where built-in device types, error recovery, and config management make things much faster and less error-prone. Both can be combined, for example, Netmiko for device config, Paramiko for firmware uploads or custom file transfers.

Managing VLANs

VLANs are a key part of modern network design. We can use them to segment traffic, isolate departments, and improve performance and security without having to physically rewire the network. And as an automation engineer, being able to manage VLANs programmatically will save we hours and reduce the risk of configuration drift or human error.

In a real-world environment, we will often need to:

- Create, delete, or rename VLANs across dozens or hundreds of switches.
- Assign ports to VLANs for new users or devices.
- Audit existing VLAN configurations to spot misconfigurations, security risks, or unused VLANs.
- Migrate users or services between VLANs as projects and departments change.

It's a pain to update each device manually, and it's prone to errors. The automation allows us make changes consistently, validate every step, and roll back if something goes wrong.

We will now try to automate VLAN management on a Cisco switch. We will make use of Netmiko. This pattern is nearly identical for other vendors, as we simply have to adjust the **`device_type`** and command syntax.

First, we will create a VLAN:

```
from netmiko import ConnectHandler
device = {
    'device_type': 'cisco_ios',
    'ip': '192.168.56.101',
    'username': 'admin',
    'password': 'mypass'
}
conn = ConnectHandler(**device)
vlan_id = 120
vlan_name = "HR_Segmentation"
commands = [
    f'vlan {vlan_id}',
    f'name {vlan_name}',
    'exit'
]
output = conn.send_config_set(commands)
print(output)
conn.disconnect()
```

This creates VLAN 120 and names it. It's idempotent, if VLAN 120 exists, it just updates the name.

We then try to assign a port to this VLAN:

```
interface = 'GigabitEthernet1/0/5'
commands = [
    f'interface {interface}',
    f'switchport access vlan {vlan_id}',
    'exit'
]
output = conn.send_config_set(commands)
```

```
print(output)
```

We then need to run an auditing of the VLANs:

```
output = conn.send_command('show vlan brief')
print(output)
```

We do this to compare against the source of truth, and so we can flag any discrepancies. Now, for multi-device changes, we need to loop through the device list, and wrap connections in **try/except** blocks for error resilience. If there are rollback, we need to store the previous VLAN assignments before making changes, so we can restore state if needed.

Executing Remote Commands

On a network, the fastest way to learn what's really happening is to run real commands, collect live results, and react in real time. We already know how to open SSH sessions. So here in this topic, we will learn to build a routine where our scripts talk to devices, run the exact commands we want, grab results, and make our daily tasks almost automatic.

Suppose the boss drops a ticket asking, "Can we check the NTP status and show interfaces on every router in Building C?" Doing this by hand, device by device, is a recipe for mistakes and late nights. We are going to automate it instead. But before we run anything, we need two things, a list of devices and a list of commands. So, we create a **devices.csv** file. Every device we might need to reach, its IP, device type, username, and password, goes here. It's like the personal inventory.

```
ip,device_type,username,password
10.10.10.1,cisco_ios,admin,YourSecret1
10.10.10.2,cisco_ios,admin,YourSecret2
```

And the commands for the day? Maybe we just jot them in a text file, **commands.txt**:

```
show ntp status
show interfaces
```

And it keeps our script flexible, so we can add more devices or new commands if we want. The only thing we need to do is update a file, and we are all set.

Reading Inventory and Commands

So now we begin. Here, at first, we pull in all the devices and commands.

```
import csv
devices = []
with open('devices.csv') as devfile:
    reader = csv.DictReader(devfile)
    for row in reader:
        devices.append(row)
with open('commands.txt') as cmdfile:
    commands = [line.strip() for line in cmdfile if
line.strip()]
```

Now here, the **devices** is a list of dictionaries, and **commands** is just a list of what we want to run.

Connecting, Running, and Saving Outputs

Now in this step, this program becomes more interactive. For each device, the script connects, runs each command, grabs the output, and saves it to a timestamped log file, so we can review or share later.

```
from netmiko import ConnectHandler
import time
for device in devices:
    print(f"Working on {device['ip']}...")
    try:
        conn = ConnectHandler(
            device_type=device['device_type'],
            ip=device['ip'],
            username=device['username'],
            password=device['password']
        )
        for cmd in commands:
            print(f"Running '{cmd}'...")
            output = conn.send_command(cmd)
```

```
            timestamp = time.strftime('%Y%m%d-%H%M%S')
            fname = f"{device['ip']}_{cmd.replace(' ',
'_')}_{timestamp}.log"
            with open(fname, 'w') as logfile:
                logfile.write(output)
            print(f"Saved output to {fname}")
        conn.disconnect()
        print(f"Done with {device['ip']}\n")
    except Exception as err:
        print(f"Could not finish {device['ip']}: {err}")
```

In the above, every step is visible. If a device is down, if a command fails, if we mistype something, the script tells us immediately, and moves on.

Automate Problem Identification

When we are doing that, don't just stop at collecting outputs. If there's an issue, like NTP is out of sync or a link is down, have the script look for keywords and flag them right off the bat.

```
if 'unsynchronized' in output:
    print(f"NTP problem detected on {device['ip']}! Fix this
soon.")
```

We can send an email or a Slack notification right from the script, anything to get the attention when it matters.

Parallelizing

If we have got an entire campus, we want to go through all the devices at once, not wait for each to finish. We can achieve that with a **ThreadPoolExecutor**. It allows us work on a bunch of them at the same time as shown below:

```
from concurrent.futures import ThreadPoolExecutor
def run_commands(device):
    # (as above)
    pass
with ThreadPoolExecutor(max_workers=5) as pool:
```

```
    pool.map(run_commands, devices)
```

We can pick **max_workers**, 5, 10, 20, based on how busy we want the machine and network to get.

Handling Unexpected Prompts

There are some commands that might pause and wait for confirmation. So here, we can make use of Netmiko's **send_command_timing()** so the script "presses Enter" or answers 'y' for you:

```
output = conn.send_command_timing('reload')
if 'confirm' in output:
    output += conn.send_command_timing('\n')
print(output)
```

With this, no stuck scripts and no more manual interventions.

Retrieving & Modifying Device Configuration

For me, this is where automation really shines. It's not like logging in, running show run, copy-pasting outputs, and hoping we didn't miss something. Instead, we have to build scripts that back up every config, every day, every device, and then able to spot drift right away and make changes only where we want, with full control.

Automated Backup

We may not be aware of but every good network engineer keeps a backup. And here, we will try to make it automatic. We can simply tell the script to connect, run **show running-config**, and save the result with the device IP and date.

```
for device in devices:
    try:
        conn = ConnectHandler(**device)
        output = conn.send_command('show running-config')
        timestamp = time.strftime('%Y%m%d-%H%M%S')
        fname = f"{device['ip']}_backup_{timestamp}.txt"
        with open(fname, 'w') as backup:
```

```
            backup.write(output)
        print(f"Config saved for {device['ip']}")
        conn.disconnect()
    except Exception as e:
        print(f"Backup failed for {device['ip']}: {e}")
```

After this, there will be no missing backups, and no more "Oops, I lost that config."

Detecting Changes

Whenever we back up, do a comparison of today's configuration with yesterdays. The python's **difflib** makes it a supercool breeze.

```
import difflib
with open('old_config.txt') as old, open('new_config.txt') as new:
    diff = difflib.unified_diff(old.readlines(), new.readlines())
    print(''.join(diff))
```

We can instantly see what's changed, like added VLANs, missing lines, typo fixes. If something unexpected appears, we then need to examine it before it becomes a bigger problem.

Pushing Changes

And if we need to update an interface description or add a new VLAN, we can do that too. The first step is to prepare the commands, push them, and then double-check the result.

```
commands = [
    'interface GigabitEthernet1/0/1',
    'description Connected to R&D Printer',
    'exit'
]
conn.send_config_set(commands)
conn.save_config()  # save to memory if the device supports it
print("Change applied.")
```

If we make a mistake, we have still got the backup, and can restore in seconds.

Rollback

Whatever we do, when we push a change, make sure we have a backup from right before. If a new config causes problems, just restore the last good version. There are some platforms (like Juniper) that support **`rollback`** natively. In some cases, the script can re-apply the backup using the same logic as pushing new configs. This includes every command, backup, and change, as well as keeping logs with the device IP, timestamp, and action. And with Git, we can keep track of all the config changes, so we always know who made what, when, and why.

Updating Device Firmware

Now, we're going to dive into how to **update the device firmware**. This is very important for fixing security issues, adding new features, and keeping the support contracts valid. But unlike changing a config, a firmware update can take a device offline, reset settings, or even brick it if something goes wrong. That's where automation comes in. It cuts down on manual steps, speeds up batch upgrades, and helps we avoid costly mistakes. The manual upgrades are full of risk: typos, missed steps, and forgotten confirmations. With scripts, we document every move, repeat the same process on every device, and log results for later review. We can even schedule upgrades for quiet hours or stage them in small batches.

Standard Workflow

The updation of the firmware always involves the following steps:

1. ***Upload the new firmware image*** to the device (often using SFTP, SCP, or TFTP).
2. ***Verify the upload*** by checking the file size or hash.
3. ***Set the boot variable*** or instruct the device to use the new image on next reboot.
4. ***Save the config*** and reload or reboot the device.
5. ***Check device status after reboot***, making sure the new version is running and all key services are up.

Uploading Firmware

Most of the modern devices will allows us to transfer files via SFTP or SCP. Let's consider that we have a Cisco switch and we will try to automate the upload in the following steps:

- Using Netmiko (for SCP):

```
from netmiko import ConnectHandler, file_transfer
device = {
    'device_type': 'cisco_ios',
```

```
    'ip': '10.0.0.101',
    'username': 'admin',
    'password': 'mypass'
}
conn = ConnectHandler(**device)
transfer_result = file_transfer(
    conn,
    source_file='cat9k_iosxe.17.09.03.SPA.bin',
    dest_file='cat9k_iosxe.17.09.03.SPA.bin',
    file_system='flash:',
    direction='put',
    overwrite_file=True
)
if transfer_result['file_exists'] and
transfer_result['file_verified']:
    print("Firmware uploaded and verified.")
else:
    print("Upload failed, check logs.")
conn.disconnect()
```

- Using Paramiko (for SFTP):

```
import paramiko
ssh = paramiko.SSHClient()
ssh.set_missing_host_key_policy(paramiko.AutoAddPolicy())
ssh.connect('10.0.0.101', username='admin', password='mypass')
sftp = ssh.open_sftp()
sftp.put('cat9k_iosxe.17.09.03.SPA.bin',
'/flash/cat9k_iosxe.17.09.03.SPA.bin')
sftp.close()
ssh.close()
```

```
print("Firmware image uploaded via SFTP.")
```

But before we do that, make sure we double-check the file name, the destination path, and how much space is available.

Setting Boot Variables

Once the image is uploaded, we need to tell the device to boot from it next time.

```
boot_command = 'boot system
flash:cat9k_iosxe.17.09.03.SPA.bin'
conn = ConnectHandler(**device)
conn.send_config_set([boot_command])
conn.save_config()
print("Boot variable set.")
```

With this level of automation, we are able to turn what used to be an all-night project into a reliable, repeatable task, even across dozens or hundreds of devices. And do not forget that the every prgoram run just gets easier and safer as we continue to improve the scripts.

Summary

Throughout this chapter, we explored why network automation matters and got hands-on with the tools and workflows that make real automation possible. We learned how to use Netmiko and Paramiko to manage devices over SSH, configure VLANs, build scripts for parallel connections, and handle the quirks and prompts that real networks throw the way.

We then practiced automating command execution at scale, retrieving and backing up device configurations, detecting drift, and applying changes safely. We also got the hands-on of firmware upgrades, how to stage, upload, verify, and trigger the reboots, all with checks and safety nets built in. With all such learnings, we really moved from basic scripts to robust, production-ready automation, able to adapt and scale the solutions for any network.

CHAPTER 5: NETWORK MONITORING AND ANALYSIS

Chapter Overview

This chapter will teach we how to build a practical, Python-powered network monitoring system from the ground up. We will see how SNMP makes it possible to check device health, monitor interfaces, and spot problems before they grow. As we go through the exercises, we will get hands-on experience with live stats, collecting and analyzing traffic data, and running throughput and latency tests with professional tools like iperf3 and ping3. We will learn real-world techniques for packet capture, traffic analysis, and automated alerting. Then, we will combine them into a unified workflow that helps we keep the network fast, reliable, and secure. By the time we are done with this chapter, we will have scripts and methods for turning raw network data into useful information, ready to solve real problems, justify upgrades, and keep every device in top shape.

Understanding Network Monitoring & Analysis

Whenever we operate or secure any real-world network, the most powerful ally is visibility. We want to know, at every moment, which devices are up or down, where bottlenecks are forming, and whether someone or something is putting the infrastructure at risk. The concept of network monitoring and analysis together gives us this kind of superpower, not just to react when things break, but to predict and prevent problems before they ever hit the users.

What Network Monitoring Really Means?

It's basically like asking, "Is my network up and running?" all the time. This isn't just about uptime. It keeps an eye on the CPU and memory, check the bandwidth and error rates on the interfaces, spots traffic surges, keeps a log of every device that's joining or leaving, and even scans for any suspicious patterns. We will see routers, switches, firewalls, servers and wireless access points as part of one living system.

In practice, the network monitoring splits into these areas:

- ***Performance Monitoring:*** Are devices running fast and stable? Any slowdowns or errors?
- ***Fault Monitoring:*** Is anything broken, offline, or sending alerts?
- ***Security Monitoring:*** Is someone probing for weaknesses, or has a device been compromised?
- ***Traffic Monitoring:*** How much, and what kind of data, is moving? Where are the top "talkers" and the heavy flows?

What About Network Analysis?

Monitoring is all about real-time health, while network analysis digs into patterns. We capture packets, analyze flows, find long-term trends, and identify who talks to whom and how often. This helps we tune performance, spot anomalies, and plan for growth.

One might start with SNMP to check CPU spikes, and make use of the packet capture tools like Wireshark or Scapy to trace issues, and then log all this into a time-series database for long-term analytics and dashboards. In fact, we don't need expensive, black-box tools for all this. With Python, we can script everything, like:

- Pull live stats with SNMP and the PySNMP library.
- Capture, filter, and analyze packets with Scapy.
- Check interface stats or run show commands on dozens of switches using Netmiko.
- Monitor for outages or security incidents, then alert by email, Slack, or the ticketing system.
- Collect long-term trends and visualize with Matplotlib, Seaborn, or Grafana.

In this chapter, we'll focus on the real code and workflows that network engineers and SREs actually use, so every technique fits into the automation toolkit and builds on what we have already learned.

Exploring SNMP

SNMP (Simple Network Management Protocol) is pretty much everywhere, right from the datacenter switches and routers to printers, UPSes, and wireless controllers. The main job here is making data about device health and performance available, so we can see interface counters, temperatures, fan speeds, ARP tables, routing info, and sometimes change device settings remotely.

Key Concepts

We could have probably seen SNMP "communities" in config files, these are like usernames/passwords. The SNMP comes in three major flavors:

- ***SNMPv1*** which is original, simple, but insecure (plaintext).
- ***SNMPv2c*** is another which adds more commands, still plaintext.
- ***SNMPv3*** is the last one which adds authentication, encryption, and much stronger security.

Now, most of the networks use v2c for read-only data, but SNMPv3 is the gold standard for anything sensitive or write-enabled. We must also understand that the SNMP has following elements, like:

- ***Agent*** which is the device being managed (router, switch, etc.).
- ***Manager*** is the system that queries the agent (your script, monitoring server).
- ***MIB (Management Information Base)*** is basically the "dictionary" of all possible variables we can read or set. And,
- ***OIDs (Object Identifiers)*** are unique addresses for every stat, think of these as GPS coordinates inside the device's brain.

SNMP Operations using PySNMP

Whenever we want to check the health of the routers, switches, or even environmental sensors, SNMP is the "remote control." With just a few lines of code, we can check if a link is up, find out how much traffic passed through an interface, or even flip a setting in an emergency. PySNMP makes this universal, scriptable, and cross-platform.

The **pysnmp** is a pure-Python library that works cross-platform, no C dependencies, and is actively maintained. It can perform all SNMP actions, such as the GET (read a variable), SET (change a value), WALK (browse a section of the MIB), TRAP (receive alerts), and more.

SNMP GET (Grabbing a Single Stat)

Just think of SNMP GET as asking, "What is the current temperature of this switch?" or "How many errors on port 3?" In Python, this is the starting point for all monitoring scripts.

The next question coming to the mind is how do we use it?

So here, we need three things:

- The device's IP address
- The community string ("password") for read access
- The OID (Object Identifier) for the stat we want

In the following sample, we want to check the system description (like its hostname and OS):

```
pip install pysnmp
from pysnmp.hlapi import *
ip = 'demo.snmplabs.com'
community = 'public'
oid = '1.3.6.1.2.1.1.1.0'  # sysDescr.0
iterator = getCmd(
    SnmpEngine(),
    CommunityData(community),
    UdpTransportTarget((ip, 161)),
    ContextData(),
    ObjectType(ObjectIdentity(oid))
)
errorIndication, errorStatus, errorIndex, varBinds =
next(iterator)
```

```
if errorIndication:
    print("Error:", errorIndication)
elif errorStatus:
    print(f"SNMP error: {errorStatus.prettyPrint()}")
else:
    for varBind in varBinds:
        print(f"Result: {varBind[0]} = {varBind[1]}")
```

We can swap in any OID to pull any stat: CPU usage, temperature, link state, memory free, whatever the devices support.

SNMP WALK (Gathering a Whole Table)

Sometimes, we don't know how many interfaces, VLANs, or ARP entries we will find. SNMP WALK "walks" a branch of the device's MIB and collects everything under that branch.

In the following example, we will list all interface names:

```
from pysnmp.hlapi import *
ip = 'demo.snmplabs.com'
community = 'public'
base_oid = '1.3.6.1.2.1.2.2.1.2'  # ifDescr
for (errorIndication, errorStatus, errorIndex, varBinds) in
nextCmd(
    SnmpEngine(),
    CommunityData(community),
    UdpTransportTarget((ip, 161)),
    ContextData(),
    ObjectType(ObjectIdentity(base_oid)),
    lexicographicMode=False
):
    if errorIndication:
        print("Error:", errorIndication)
        break
```

```
    elif errorStatus:
        print(f"SNMP error: {errorStatus.prettyPrint()}")
        break
    else:
        for varBind in varBinds:
            print(f"{varBind[0]} = {varBind[1]}")
```

Using the SNMP WALK, we can build live inventories, check every interface's status, or watch traffic on all ports. If we monitor, say, bandwidth on all uplinks, a single script can collect all the data in one sweep.

SNMP SET (Changing Device State)

The SNMP SET isn't just reading, it's writing. Let us think that we want to update the "contact" info on every switch, or even reset an interface. The SNMP SET is used here but, we must use only if we know exactly what will change.

Following is an example where we are setting an SNMP contact string:

```
from pysnmp.hlapi import *
ip = 'demo.snmplabs.com'
community = 'private'  # Typically write access
oid = '1.3.6.1.2.1.1.4.0'  # sysContact.0
iterator = setCmd(
    SnmpEngine(),
    CommunityData(community, mpModel=0),
    UdpTransportTarget((ip, 161)),
    ContextData(),
    ObjectType(ObjectIdentity(oid), 'admin@yourdomain.com')
)
errorIndication, errorStatus, errorIndex, varBinds =
next(iterator)
if errorIndication:
    print("Error:", errorIndication)
elif errorStatus:
```

```
    print(f"SNMP error: {errorStatus.prettyPrint()}")
else:
    for varBind in varBinds:
        print(f"Set result: {varBind[0]} = {varBind[1]}")
```

Now here, the device may reject the change if we use the wrong community, wrong OID, or try to change a read-only field. This needs to be test on lab gear first!

SNMP TRAP (Catching Alerts Instantly)

This particualar SNMP sets a trap that let devices tell we when something changes. This includes power loss, interface down, overheating, and so on. With PySNMP, we can receive these alerts and trigger instant responses.

Following is a sample program that establishes a basic trap receiver:

```
from pysnmp.carrier.asyncore.dgram import udp
from pysnmp.entity import engine, config
from pysnmp.entity.rfc3413 import ntfrcv
snmpEngine = engine.SnmpEngine()
config.addTransport(
    snmpEngine,
    udp.domainName,
    udp.UdpTransport().openServerMode(('0.0.0.0', 162))
)
config.addV1System(snmpEngine, 'my-area', 'public')
def cbFun(snmpEngine, stateReference, contextEngineId,
contextName, varBinds, cbCtx):
    print("Received SNMP Trap:")
    for varBind in varBinds:
        print(' = '.join([x.prettyPrint() for x in varBind]))
ntfrcv.NotificationReceiver(snmpEngine, cbFun)
print("Listening for SNMP traps on port 162...")
snmpEngine.transportDispatcher.jobStarted(1)
```

```
snmpEngine.transportDispatcher.runDispatcher()
```

Using such traps, we don't have to poll every device constantly. Setting this, the devices push alerts to you, so we can respond right away, perfect for high-priority issues.

Network Traffic Monitoring

The concept of network traffic monitoring is all about "seeing" what's really flowing through the cables and airwaves. That way, we can spot bottlenecks, detect unexpected spikes, and decide smarter about upgrades, security, and troubleshooting. And with Python, we are not stuck with premade dashboards. We can script the exact monitoring routines we need.

Approach of Traffic Monitoring

At the core, the concept of monitoring network traffic comes down to either polling device counters (like bytes in/out on each interface) or actually sniffing live packets as they pass the interface. And, each method has its role.

Polling Device Counters

We have already seen in the previous topic about how the SNMP makes it easy to grab interface statistics. Now here for traffic monitoring, we can poll OIDs like **ifInOctets** and **ifOutOctets** to measure the number of bytes or packets moving through a port over time.

Now to the best of my knowledge, we can follow a common pattern, like:

- Grab the byte counter now
- Wait a fixed interval (say, 60 seconds)
- Grab the counter again
- Subtract the first value from the second
- Divide by the interval to get bytes per second

Following is a quick example (bytes in per second):

```
import time
from pysnmp.hlapi import *
def get_bytes_in(ip, community, oid):
    iterator = getCmd(
        SnmpEngine(),
        CommunityData(community),
        UdpTransportTarget((ip, 161)),
```

```
        ContextData(),
        ObjectType(ObjectIdentity(oid))
    )
    errorIndication, errorStatus, errorIndex, varBinds =
next(iterator)
    for varBind in varBinds:
        return int(varBind[1])
ip = 'demo.snmplabs.com'
community = 'public'
oid = '1.3.6.1.2.1.2.2.1.10.2'  # ifInOctets for interface 2
start = get_bytes_in(ip, community, oid)
time.sleep(60)
end = get_bytes_in(ip, community, oid)
bps = (end - start) / 60
print(f"Bytes in per second: {bps}")
```

Sniffing Live Packets

If we need to see what kind of packets are traversing the network, protocols, sources, destinations, Python's **scapy** library is the gold standard for live packet capture.

For this, we first install scapy:

```
pip install scapy
```

Then we can simply run the basic packet sniff:

```
from scapy.all import sniff
def process_packet(packet):
    print(packet.summary())
sniff(prn=process_packet, count=10)  # Capture 10 packets,
then stop
```

Here, we can filter by interface, protocol, or even custom conditions. This is especially useful for spotting security threats or debugging a tricky service issue.

Once we have time-series data (from SNMP or packet counters), we can then visualize it using

Python's **matplotlib**, **seaborn**, or even stream it to a tool like Grafana or InfluxDB for real-time dashboards.

Measuring Network Performance

The performance of the networks isn't just about bandwidth. There are other things, such as latency (how long it takes for a packet to travel), jitter (variation in delay), packet loss, and reliability over time. If we measure them, we can spot problems before users do, and it guides upgrades and fixes.

ICMP Ping

A simple and reliable way to test connectivity and latency is to use ICMP ping. There are python libraries like **ping3** that make this easy.

If we want to measure latency, we can run the following sample script:

```
pip install ping3
from ping3 import ping
host = '8.8.8.8'
latency = ping(host)
if latency is not None:
    print(f"Ping latency to {host}: {latency*1000:.2f} ms")
else:
    print(f"Host {host} is unreachable.")
```

We can run this test a few times, collect some samples, and calculate things like average latency, jitter, that's the variation between results, and packet loss, how often the ping fails.

Advanced Testing using 'iperf3'

For real throughput and performance tests, I recommend to make use of **iperf3** which is the professional standard in my opinion. We can automate it with Python using the **iperf3** package through the following program:

```
pip install iperf3
import iperf3
client = iperf3.Client()
```

```
client.server_hostname = 'your.iperf3.server.ip'
client.port = 5201
result = client.run()
if result.error:
    print("Test failed:", result.error)
else:
    print(f"Sent {result.sent_Mbps:.2f} Mbps | Received {result.received_Mbps:.2f} Mbps")
```

This sets up an iperf3 server on the other end, and the script runs throughput tests, records bandwidth, and logs any errors.

Both these scripts help we prevent outages and prove when the network is performing well.

Analyzing Network Performance

It's all about turning those numbers into useful insights when we are dealing with raw monitoring data, bytes, latency, jitter, throughput, and loss. Is the network fast enough? Are there any patterns or bottlenecks? Should we upgrade, optimize, or troubleshoot further? That's where performance analysis comes in. We've already collected live data using SNMP, ping, and iperf3, and now we'll learn how to interpret it, identify real issues, and communicate them with clear evidence.

Analysis Approach

First, think about trends, thresholds, and anomalies. The ***Trends*** show we how metrics evolve over time. Are things getting worse? Improving? Next, then check the ***Thresholds*** that help we define what's normal and what's not. Exceeding them signals a problem, maybe bandwidth is too low, or latency is too high. And, then the ***Anomalies*** which points us to sudden changes: a spike in traffic, a jump in latency, or a sudden burst of dropped packets.

Analysis Workflow

We first gather the data and collect the SNMP counters, latency results from ping, throughput from iperf3, or packet captures using eith Scapy or Wireshark. After this, we then make use of the Python's **matplotlib** or **seaborn** to chart time-series data. In this, even a simple line chart can reveal congestion periods or a slow upward drift in errors.

```
import matplotlib.pyplot as plt
times = ["10:00", "10:05", "10:10"]
```

```
latencies = [12.3, 19.8, 21.2]
plt.plot(times, latencies, marker='o')
plt.title("Ping Latency Over Time")
plt.xlabel("Time")
plt.ylabel("Latency (ms)")
plt.show()
```

While doing this, we need to analyze our collected data for average, median, min, and max values. We need to set thresholds for what we consider "healthy", for example, "latency above 50 ms triggers a warning." When we see a sudden spike or drop, it is a sign that we need to dig in. We need to compare against known maintenance windows, or check device logs and traffic patterns. Sometimes, we may see a big spike which means a backup ran or someone downloaded a huge file. Other times, it signals a hardware or link failure.

Let's say we are keeping an eye on the interface counters every five minutes and we see the rate shoot up from 100 Mbps to 990 Mbps. As soon as that happens, we will also see higher ping latency and packet drops to that switch. We put two and two together, see that the link is maxed out, and now we have got the info we need to plan an upgrade or figure out what's using up all that bandwidth.

Summary

Throughout this chapter, we learned how to design and script network monitoring, traffic capture, and performance testing. We explored SNMP with PySNMP, polled devices for live stats, walked MIB tables, and even made configuration changes remotely. We automated bandwidth and error monitoring, practiced live packet capture with Scapy, and set up throughput and latency testing using ping3 and iperf3.

With every technique, we learned not just to gather data, but to visualize and interpret it, spotting trends, identifying thresholds, and catching anomalies before they affect users. By using Python, we built routines that run automatically, alert us to real issues, and keep records for compliance or optimization. Every workflow focused on moving from raw data to actionable insight, so we can troubleshoot, tune, and defend the network with facts instead of guesswork.

CHAPTER 6: NETWORK SECURITY AND PYTHON

Chapter Overview

In this chapter, we will explore the essential building blocks and day-to-day practices of network security for both traditional and cloud-native environments. This chapter will make we think like an attacker and a defender, building layered security from firewalls and vulnerability scanning to advanced intrusion detection and secure communications.

Moving forward, we will learn to automate the configuration, enforcement, and auditing of security controls using Python, making best practices repeatable and reliable. Nexrt, we will then explore the latest standards for SSL/TLS, script audits to ensure every endpoint meets encryption requirements, and handle certificate management at scale. We will gain experience integrating IDS/IPS tools and using packet analysis libraries like Scapy to spot and respond to threats in real time. And finally, we will then understand how to securely establish, monitor, and manage VPN connections, extending the secure perimeter wherever business requires.

Setting up Firewall

It's all about enforcing the network's security policy, and firewalls are often the best bet. No matter if we are dealing with a hardware appliance in a data center or a built-in software firewall on a Linux server, the idea is always the same. Firewalls are like gatekeepers, deciding which traffic is allowed in or out based on the rules we set. These rules might allow web traffic to the public server, block management ports from outside, or only allow SSH from certain subnets. When we combine these controls, we are able to reduce the "attack surface" exposed to the world, making it much harder for threats to slip through unnoticed. The key here isn't just writing rules, but making sure they're accurate, up to date, and automatically enforced across all devices. We can do manual configuration for a single server, but in a real environment, we want automation because it's consistent and fast.

It's all hands-on with firewalls, so we learn to tweak the rules and see what happens to real traffic. For most modern Linux systems, iptables or nftables are the go-to for the firewall. We can manage these interactively or with automation. Let's say we want to allow SSH connections only from the office subnet. We can use Python-iptables to create a script that adds an "accept" rule for TCP port 22 from the trusted range and a "drop" rule for everything else. This saves we time and helps prevent mistakes that might happen if we were copying and pasting commands at 2 a.m. during an emergency.

Following is a real-world example:

```
import iptc
def allow_ssh_from(src_ip):
    rule = iptc.Rule()
```

```
    rule.src = src_ip
    rule.protocol = "tcp"
    match = rule.create_match("tcp")
    match.dport = "22"
    rule.target = iptc.Target(rule, "ACCEPT")
    chain = iptc.Chain(iptc.Table(iptc.Table.FILTER), "INPUT")
    chain.insert_rule(rule)
allow_ssh_from("10.0.0.0/24")
```

This above script makes the SSH access policy repeatable and auditable. In the same program, we can pull a list of allowed IPs from a configuration file, or automatically remove rules at the end of a maintenance window, or add new blocks if we detect brute-force attempts.

From my personal experience, one of the most important habits we will develop is always testing firewall rules in a lab or on a non-critical system first. It's far too easy to lock yourself out of a remote server with one wrong rule, so we must have always the console access, or an alternative back door, before we apply changes in production. And because firewalls can "forget" rules after a reboot (unless we make them persistent), always save the working configurations. There are tools like **`iptables-persistent`**, or the built-in **`firewalld`**, to reload the rules automatically at startup.

Scanning Network Vulnerability

When we manage networks of any size, vulnerability scanning acts as the early warning system. Rather than waiting for attackers to find the holes, we systematically scan the infrastructure for open ports, exposed services, outdated firmware, and misconfigurations that attackers exploit. The concept of implementing the vulnerability scanning is not a one-time job, it's a cycle that must repeat regularly as the network changes, new devices join, and software updates bring new risks. This helps to identify weaknesses before they become security incidents. This gives us time to fix issues on the terms, rather than racing to respond after a breach. A strong scanning routine also help we demonstrate compliance with security standards and pass customer or auditor reviews.

We must know that a robust scanning workflow blends both automated and manual approaches. There are well-known tools like ***Nmap*** let us sweep large address ranges, fingerprint devices, and test for thousands of vulnerabilities using community-developed scripts. We can automate these with Python, so the scans run on a schedule, save results, and even trigger alerts if new risks appear.

Following is a sample pattern with the help of **`python-nmap`**:

```
import nmap
scanner = nmap.PortScanner()
scanner.scan('192.168.1.0/24', arguments='-sV --script vuln')
for host in scanner.all_hosts():
    print(f"Host: {host}")
    for proto in scanner[host].all_protocols():
        for port in scanner[host][proto]:
            state = scanner[host][proto][port]['state']
            print(f"  Port: {port}\tState: {state}")
```

here, we may bring in some more specialized tools like ***OpenVAS*** for vulnerability databases or ***Nessus*** for compliance reporting.

The goal is to be proactive and regular with the scans, not reactive. During off-hours, we suggest running broad scans to keep things running smoothly and focusing targeted scans on sensitive assets or public-facing services. After each scan, compare the results to previous ones to find any new or unresolved issues. When we combine scanning with patch management and change control, we can rest assured that the network's risk is constantly diminishing, not escalating. The goal isn't just to find weaknesses, but to fix them fast and show the company's dedication to real, ongoing security.

Secure Communication with SSL/TLS

Every time data crosses the network, it faces the risk of interception, theft, or tampering. The SSL and its successor TLS provide the encryption and authentication needed to secure everything from web pages and APIs to remote management sessions. With these protocols, we prevent eavesdroppers from reading sensitive information, and we ensure that both sides of a conversation are truly who they claim to be. The proper SSL/TLS usage has become the expectation for every serious service, browsers warn users about insecure connections, and compliance standards demand strong encryption everywhere. But security is only as strong as the implementation: old protocols, weak ciphers, or expired certificates leave dangerous gaps, even if we think we are protected.

The python's **`ssl`** and **`socket`** modules give us the power to inspect, validate, and automate SSL/TLS for any networked application. With just a few lines of code, we can connect to a remote service, check which TLS version is in use, review the certificate authority chain, and verify expiration dates.

Following is a sample program to carry out the basic check:

```
import ssl, socket
hostname = 'www.example.com'
context = ssl.create_default_context()
with socket.create_connection((hostname, 443)) as sock:
    with context.wrap_socket(sock, server_hostname=hostname)
as ssock:
        print(ssock.version())
        print(ssock.getpeercert())
```

Now this program can be easily expanded to scan every other domain the company owns and alert we about certificates expiring soon, or audit all services to ensure only the latest TLS versions are enabled. If combined with **requests** or other HTTP libraries, we enforce strong, validated HTTPS connections in all the API calls and service integrations.

Exploring Scapy

When we need to go beyond off-the-shelf tools and truly "see" or manipulate packets on the wire, ***Scapy*** is the Python-powered microscope, Swiss Army knife, and packet-forging forge, all in one. It allows us capture, craft, dissect, and replay network packets at nearly any protocol layer, all with interactive scripts and instant feedback. Unlike higher-level libraries (such as those for HTTP, FTP, or SNMP), it doesn't just talk to protocols, it allows us build them from scratch, probe for weaknesses, automate custom attacks, or debug complex issues when nothing else will do.

The Scapy is widely used for tasks like traffic sniffing, network discovery, custom traceroutes, fuzzing, and security research. We can use it to scan for devices (ARP or ICMP discovery), test firewall rules by sending crafted packets, analyze DNS responses for anomalies, or even simulate attacks (with permission, of course) to test the IDS/IPS configuration. Its syntax is remarkably readable, making packet crafting and manipulation not just powerful, but also accessible to those just starting in security.

Now to begin using Scapy, we can first get it installed using pip:

```
pip install scapy
```

Now here, ket us say that we want to sniff live traffic and analyze HTTP requests passing through the interface. Following script can easily capture and print the summary information:

```
from scapy.all import sniff
def show_packet(packet):
```

```
    print(packet.summary())
sniff(filter="tcp port 80", prn=show_packet, count=10)
```

To tell we in detail, it captures ten HTTP packets, calling the custom function each time a new one arrives. We can easily change the filter or add logic to parse payloads, detect anomalies, or log results to a file. Similarly, what if we want to send a custom packet, such as, a crafted ICMP echo request to test network reachability or security controls. Then here,

```
from scapy.all import IP, ICMP, send
packet = IP(dst="8.8.8.8")/ICMP()
send(packet)
print("Custom ICMP packet sent.")
```

This program can generate packets for any protocol we can think of. It supports TCP, UDP, DNS, and even some of the less common ones, like GRE or IGMP. We can manipulate every field, inject anomalies, or create fuzzed input for security testing. So, whether we are looking into a possible breach, doing a penetration test, or just figuring out how these protocols really work, Scapy's the tool for you. It gives us full control over every byte and bit.

Establishing VPNs

Once we have got the basics covered—like setting up the firewalls, tuning the IDS/IPS, and making sure all the traffic is encrypted with SSL/TLS—the next thing we should think about is how to securely connect remote users, branch offices, and cloud workloads over the public internet. We can use a VPN—that's a Virtual Private Network—to do this without giving up the privacy or control. A VPN can help make the users and remote networks part of the secure perimeter. It does this by using authentication, encryption, and access controls. This keeps outsiders out and the data private. Basically, this means that every packet traveling between endpoints is wrapped in a secure tunnel. This tunnel is invisible to attackers and safe from tampering.

So now, we will deploy a site-to-site or remote-access VPN using ***OpenVPN*** and ***WireGuard***. Both these are the widely respected options, and both of them can be managed and orchestrated with Python.

Automated Deployment of OpenVPN

To begin with, we first get the openvpn installed:

```
sudo apt update
```

```
sudo apt install openvpn easy-rsa
```

After thids, we then initialize a PKI for secure authentication:

```
make-cadir ~/openvpn-ca
cd ~/openvpn-ca
source vars
./clean-all
./build-ca
./build-key-server server
./build-dh
./build-key client1
./build-key client2
```

This sequence creates certificate/key pairs for both the server and each client. The python can automate certificate generation and deployment with **subprocess**, templating, and secure file transfer (using **paramiko**).

Now what if we want to automate configuration pushes and restarts when adding a new user? We can do this through the following program:

```
import subprocess
import paramiko
def deploy_new_client(server_ip, username):
    # Generate new key/cert locally
    subprocess.run(["./build-key", username])
    # Use paramiko to transfer files
    ssh = paramiko.SSHClient()
    ssh.set_missing_host_key_policy(paramiko.AutoAddPolicy())
    ssh.connect(server_ip, username='ubuntu')
    sftp = ssh.open_sftp()
    sftp.put(f'keys/{username}.crt',
f'/etc/openvpn/clients/{username}.crt')
    sftp.close()
```

```
    ssh.exec_command('sudo systemctl restart openvpn@server')
    ssh.close()
    print(f"Deployed new VPN client: {username}")
deploy_new_client('10.0.0.10', 'alice')
```

This above line of codes will automate tedious manual steps and will ensure to keep the VPN user management consistent and repeatable.

Deploying WireGuard

The WireGuard is a newer, high-performance VPN known for its minimal config and speed. To continue our program, we will generate the key pairs for server and clients, and prior to it, we will also install the WireGuard:

```
sudo apt install wireguard
wg genkey | tee server_private.key | wg pubkey >
server_public.key
wg genkey | tee client_private.key | wg pubkey >
client_public.key
```

Following is a sample server config:

```
[Interface]
PrivateKey = <server_private_key>
Address = 10.20.0.1/24
ListenPort = 51820
[Peer]
PublicKey = <client_public_key>
AllowedIPs = 10.20.0.2/32
```

And the following is a sample client config:

```
[Interface]
PrivateKey = <client_private_key>
Address = 10.20.0.2/32
[Peer]
```

```
PublicKey = <server_public_key>
Endpoint = <server_ip>:51820
AllowedIPs = 0.0.0.0/0
```

One interesting thing is that the python can generate both these files using string templates and automatically distribute them using SCP or cloud-init scripts for rapid deployment.

Monitoring and Validating VPN Health

A very good and intersting feature of the VPN setup is that it doesn't just connect, but it also monitors. The python scripts can run regular health checks by pinging VPN endpoints, analyzing logs for failed connections or suspicious patterns, and even automatically revoking credentials for lost/stolen devices.

Given below is an example of a script to check the VPN connectivity and log the downtime:

```
import subprocess
import time
def check_vpn(host):
    while True:
        result = subprocess.run(['ping', '-c', '1', host],
stdout=subprocess.PIPE)
        if result.returncode == 0:
            print(f"{host} reachable")
        else:
            print(f"ALERT: {host} unreachable")
        time.sleep(300)  # Check every 5 minutes
check_vpn("10.20.0.2")
```

Now while we run the script, we need to ensure to use the strong keys, disable unused authentication modes, and restrict what each VPN user or site can access.

Summary

Throughout this chapter, we've gone over how to think about network security as a never-ending, multi-layered thing. First things first, we got to know some core security principles like defense in depth, threat modeling and the CIA triad. We learned the ropes by setting up and automating firewalls using Python, scanning for vulnerabilities with tools like Nmap, and interpreting real-world scan results.

We explored how SSL/TLS keeps communications private, audited certificates and encryption settings, and practiced automating certificate validation in Python. We took it a step further by learning about intrusion detection and prevention, integrating IDS/IPS alerts into automation workflows, and parsing real-time logs for actionable threats. We really got into Scapy, learning how to capture, craft, and analyze packets for advanced troubleshooting and security research. At last, we figured out a clear, step-by-step way to set up and keep an eye on VPNs. We learned how to make, automate, and protect private tunnels for remote access and site-to-site connections.

CHAPTER 7: WORKING WITH APIS AND NETWORK SERVICES

Chapter Overview

In this chapter, we will learn how APIs form the foundation of modern, automated network management and how Python empowers us to harness these interfaces across devices, platforms, and cloud services. We will dive deep into the fundamental API patterns, REST, SOAP, RPC, and device-specific protocols, learning both the theory and the hands-on steps needed to interact, authenticate, and automate.

As we progress, we will master the use of Python's **`requests`** and related libraries for scripting reliable interactions, handling large responses, dealing with authentication tokens, and building robust workflows. We will cover practical demonstrations to teach provisioning, monitoring, and real-time orchestration of both traditional and cloud-native infrastructure. We will see how automatic network services, like zero-touch provisioning, self-healing, and elastic scaling, can be realized with Python, APIs, and event-driven automation. By the end of this chapter, we will be equipped to design, deploy, and maintain resilient, policy-driven networks that adapt to business needs, minimize manual effort, and scale seamlessly as the environment evolves.

APIs and Their Types

APIs for Modern NetOps

When we manage or automate networks today, we are not just connecting cables or configuring routers at the console. We are orchestrating services across the cloud, managing devices at scale, collecting analytics, and integrating with other business systems, all tasks that rely on ***APIs***. APIs (Application Programming Interfaces) are the standardized doorways that let different software systems, network devices, and cloud platforms communicate. Whether we want to provision a new server, pull bandwidth stats from a switch, update DNS records, or trigger alerts, we will use APIs almost every step of the way.

Imagine a scenario where we want to check the health of a thousand network switches scattered across dozens of cities. Doing this manually would be impossible, but with APIs, we can script everything, pulling real-time stats, changing configs, or even reacting to failures automatically. That's the real power of APIs in network engineering: they make automation, integration, and rapid change not just possible, but routine.

Core API Concepts

An API defines how we ask a system for information (like a device status), what we can change (like a VLAN config), and which format data comes in (often JSON or XML). In the world of networks, APIs replace old, error-prone CLI scraping with consistent, programmable interfaces. With APIs, we don't just automate repetitive work, we make it more reliable and scalable.

A typical API interaction involves:

- ***Sending a request*** over HTTP/S, specifying the endpoint (URL), method (GET, POST, PUT, DELETE), headers, and sometimes a data payload.
- ***Receiving a response*** in JSON, XML, or plain text, containing the result, status codes, and sometimes error messages.
- ***Authenticating*** almost every API now requires authentication, API keys, tokens, or even OAuth, to secure access.

Major Types of APIs

REST APIs

The REST APIs are the backbone of most network automation today. They use standard HTTP methods, GET, POST, PUT, DELETE, to perform operations on resources identified by URLs. The REST is stateless: each request contains everything needed for the server to respond, and the server doesn't remember previous requests. That makes REST scalable, easy to test, and a top choice for cloud, device, and monitoring APIs.

Think that we want to check the interface status on a Cisco switch or add a firewall rule in AWS, both vendors provide RESTful APIs for such actions. We send a GET to **`/device/interfaces`** or a POST to **`/firewall/rules`**, pass authentication tokens in the headers, and handle the JSON response in Python.

SOAP APIs

The SOAP is older and heavier, using XML for every message and supporting a wider variety of transport protocols (HTTP, SMTP, more). It's common in legacy or enterprise systems, banking, telecom, or certain data center vendors. The SOAP supports strong standards for security, transaction handling, and reliability, making it ideal where compliance is a must, but the extra complexity means it's less favored for new projects.

If we inherit a system running on SOAP, Python's **`zeep`** library makes it possible to consume or automate those APIs, though we will deal with verbose XML and WSDL files.

XML-RPC and JSON-RPC

Both these APIs are simpler than SOAP but use similar remote procedure call models, sending requests and responses in XML or JSON. They allow direct method calls, "do this action with these arguments", across the network. While less common than REST today, we will still find XML-RPC and JSON-RPC in management platforms, monitoring tools, and open-source projects.

When we encounter legacy systems or lightweight automation tools (like certain monitoring plugins), we might need to script with these RPC APIs. The Python's **`xmlrpc.client`** or **`jsonrpcclient`** makes integration easy.

Device-level APIs

These are APIs specific to hardware vendors, routers, switches, firewalls, and more. Cisco, Juniper, Arista, and others expose REST APIs, gRPC, or proprietary endpoints that let us check device health, push config, or even perform firmware upgrades. These APIs typically provide very granular access and are much more reliable for automation than screen-scraping CLI output.

We can automate a firmware upgrade across 200 routers using the Cisco REST API, trigger the update, monitor status, and verify version, all from a single script.

GraphQL APIs

While less common in classic networking, GraphQL is gaining ground for cloud services and SDN controllers. It allows us request exactly the data structure we want, reducing bandwidth and making integrations more flexible.

Working with APIs

The python's **`requests`** library is the tool of choice for HTTP-based APIs (REST, SOAP, JSON-RPC). We send requests, pass in headers or data, and handle responses, usually in JSON. For authentication, we often add an API key or token in the headers, or use built-in methods for basic or OAuth2 auth.

Following is the live example on REST GET:

```
import requests
url = "https://api.example.com/device/status"
headers = {'Authorization': 'Bearer YOUR_TOKEN'}
response = requests.get(url, headers=headers)
response.raise_for_status()
data = response.json()
print(data)
```

The given below is the sample program on the REST POST with data:

```
import requests
url = "https://api.example.com/device/config"
headers = {'Authorization': 'Bearer YOUR_TOKEN', 'Content-
Type': 'application/json'}
```

```
payload = {'hostname': 'core-switch-01', 'vlans': [10, 20,
30]}
response = requests.post(url, headers=headers, json=payload)
print(response.json())
```

For device-specific APIs, there are Python libraries like **netmiko**, **pyntc**, or even vendor SDKs (like Cisco's **dnacentersdk**) which make it even easier to work with hardware directly, abstracting many authentication and formatting steps for you.

Once you are confident with API patterns and Python, we will be able to:

- Automate health checks and compliance reporting across hundreds of devices and services.
- Orchestrate change management, push configs, roll back, audit, and monitor at scale.
- Integrate network management with cloud, DevOps, security, and business platforms.
- Proactively detect and respond to outages, threats, or compliance issues, often before users notice.

The APIs are the "power tools" for the modern network professional. When we pair them with Python, we turn slow, manual, error-prone operations into instant, repeatable, and reliable workflows. Every hour we spend mastering these concepts will save we hundreds down the road, and keep the network secure, scalable, and future-ready.

Using Python to Interact with APIs

When we need to talk to APIs, whether it's RESTful device APIs, cloud service endpoints, or custom automation backends, the Python's **requests** library is the first and best friend, and we have learned to use it in the past chapters. All the key network automation routines, status polling, configuration changes, incident response, can be driven from this single, readable toolkit.

Making a GET Request

For example, if we want to retrieve device health data or inventory from a REST API. We'll use a GET request, pass any authentication headers, and process the JSON result.

```
import requests
url = "https://api.example.com/v1/devices"
headers = {"Authorization": "Bearer <YOUR_API_TOKEN>"}
response = requests.get(url, headers=headers)
response.raise_for_status()  # Raises error if the request
fails
```

```
devices = response.json()
for device in devices:
    print(f"{device['hostname']}: {device['status']}")
```

This code works the same way for nearly any modern API, just adjust the endpoint, headers, and fields to match the device or service.

Sending Data with POST and PUT

The APIs often expect us to send structured data, such as new configurations, policy updates, or user credentials. Most modern APIs use JSON for this.

Following is the example on creating a new VLAN:

```
import requests
import json
url = "https://api.example.com/v1/vlans"
headers = {"Authorization": "Bearer <YOUR_API_TOKEN>",
"Content-Type": "application/json"}
payload = {"id": 30, "name": "Finance", "tag": 30}
response = requests.post(url, headers=headers, json=payload)
response.raise_for_status()
print("VLAN created:", response.json())
```

In the above, we will use **PUT** or **PATCH** for updates, just as easy, but targeting a specific resource (like **/vlans/30**).

Handling Errors, Timeouts, and Rate Limits

The real-world APIs don't always behave perfectly. At times, we get timeouts, transient network issues, or "429 Too Many Requests" when we hit a rate limit. The Python's exception handling and **requests** session tools let us build resilience into the scripts.

Following is a quick example on handling errors and timeouts:

```
import requests
url = "https://api.example.com/v1/devices"
headers = {"Authorization": "Bearer <YOUR_API_TOKEN>"}
try:
```

```
    response = requests.get(url, headers=headers, timeout=10)
    response.raise_for_status()
    print(response.json())
except requests.exceptions.Timeout:
    print("Request timed out, trying again later.")
except requests.exceptions.HTTPError as err:
    print(f"API error: {err}")
```

For APIs with rate limits, many will return HTTP 429 or special headers like **`Retry-After`**. We can catch these and back off accordingly.

Authenticating APIs

A lot of APIs need you to log in. It could be as simple as an API key (in a header or URL), a bearer token (like in OAuth2 flows), or more advanced schemes.

Following is an API Key example:

```
headers = {"x-api-key": "<YOUR_KEY>"}
response = requests.get(url, headers=headers)
```

And the below is the OAuth2 Bearer Token Example (using `requests-oauthlib`):

```
from requests_oauthlib import OAuth2Session
client_id = 'YOUR_CLIENT_ID'
client_secret = 'YOUR_CLIENT_SECRET'
token_url = 'https://provider.com/oauth2/token'
oauth = OAuth2Session(client_id)
token = oauth.fetch_token(token_url, client_id=client_id,
client_secret=client_secret)
response = oauth.get('https://api.example.com/v1/devices')
print(response.json())
```

For most network automation, the API key or token will suffice, but cloud and SaaS APIs often require OAuth2 or SAML.

Pagination and Large Responses

If the API returns many results (say, hundreds or thousands of devices), results may come in "pages." We will need to follow **next** URLs or increment page numbers to retrieve the full set.

Following is the paginated API example:

```
url = "https://api.example.com/v1/devices"
headers = {"Authorization": "Bearer <YOUR_API_TOKEN>"}
while url:
    response = requests.get(url, headers=headers)
    data = response.json()
    for device in data['results']:
        print(device['hostname'])
    url = data.get('next')  # Get the next page URL, or None
```

Sessions, Retries, and Logging

For efficiency and reliability, we generally use a **requests.Session()** object to persist settings (like headers and cookies), automatically handle retries, and log all requests for debugging.

```
import requests
from requests.adapters import HTTPAdapter
from requests.packages.urllib3.util.retry import Retry
session = requests.Session()
session.headers.update({"Authorization": "Bearer
<YOUR_API_TOKEN>"})
retries = Retry(total=3, backoff_factor=1)
session.mount('https://', HTTPAdapter(max_retries=retries))
response = session.get("https://api.example.com/v1/devices")
print(response.json())
```

Here, we can also add logging with Python's **logging** module to track every API call, request body, and response code for later audit or troubleshooting.

With all these techniques, we can automate device inventory, configuration backups, policy updates, alerting, compliance checks, and more. The scripts we write for one device or platform often port easily to others, because API principles remain the same.

Automatic Network Services

Modern networks demand more than just manual configuration and monitoring. As business grows and complexity multiplies, ***automatic network services*** become the secret weapon, enabling networks to adapt, heal, scale, and even defend themselves with minimal human intervention. These services aren't just "nice to have." They are critical for zero-touch provisioning, rapid disaster recovery, seamless scaling, compliance enforcement, and keeping pace with security demands. Think about what happens when a new switch is plugged in, a cloud resource spins up, or a user requests access from a new office. If we had to handle every case by hand, bottlenecks and mistakes would soon follow. Automation bridges the gap between business agility and technical reliability.

In real environments, automatic services manifest in several ways:

- ***Zero-Touch Provisioning (ZTP):*** New devices, switches, routers, access points, can fetch configuration, firmware, and policy from a central controller the moment they come online. This slashes deployment time, reduces configuration drift, and ensures compliance. For example, a new branch router boots, sends a DHCP or API call, and instantly receives its intended settings and security posture.
- ***Self-Healing Networks:*** When an outage or anomaly is detected (like a failed link or a critical device going down), Python scripts or automation platforms detect the problem, reroute traffic, restart services, or open a ticket, often before users even notice. We can set up event-driven triggers that poll APIs, parse monitoring data, and execute recovery steps automatically.
- ***Policy-Driven Access and Security:*** Automation ensures that access controls, firewall rules, and segmentation policies update dynamically as devices and users move or change roles. For example, integration with identity providers or HR systems means that when someone's job changes, their network rights adapt instantly, no manual ACL edits required.
- ***Elastic Cloud Networking:*** In cloud or hybrid networks, automatic services enable on-demand scaling, spinning up or shutting down VPNs, firewalls, or load balancers as traffic and workloads shift. APIs from providers like AWS, Azure, and Google Cloud make this not only possible, but routine.

When it comes to making automatic services, Python is the glue that holds everything together. And we can write scripts or build workflows that:

- Listen for device onboarding events (using webhooks, SNMP traps, or log monitoring).
- Call vendor or cloud APIs to configure new devices, provision VLANs, or set up BGP peering.
- Parse monitoring data in real time, identify anomalies, and kick off remediation routines.
- Integrate with ticketing or chat platforms to alert humans only when needed, letting machines handle the rest.

Following is a practical sample of ***Auto-configuring a new switch using a REST API***:

```
import requests
def provision_switch(serial_number, config_profile):
    url = f"https://api.networkcontroller.com/v1/devices/{serial_number}/provision"
    headers = {"Authorization": "Bearer <YOUR_API_TOKEN>", "Content-Type": "application/json"}
    payload = {"profile": config_profile}
    response = requests.post(url, headers=headers, json=payload)
    if response.status_code == 200:
        print(f"Switch {serial_number} provisioned successfully.")
    else:
        print(f"Provisioning failed: {response.text}")
provision_switch("SWITCH123456789", "Branch-Standard")
```

In larger setups, there are orchestration tools like Ansible, SaltStack, or custom event-driven Python services that take these patterns and scale them across hundreds or thousands of endpoints. While automation can dramatically reduce operational overhead and error rates, it must be built on robust logic, validation, and auditing.

Summary

Throughout this chapter, we explored the world of APIs and their role in networking, gaining an in-depth understanding of REST, SOAP, device-level APIs, and authentication strategies. We learned to interact with APIs using Python's **`requests`** library, confidently crafting GET, POST, and paginated requests, managing authentication tokens, and handling errors in real-world scenarios. We have covered practical demonstrations to retrieve device inventories, push configuration changes, and process large result sets, giving us the ability to automate health checks, policy updates, and integration tasks at scale.

There were advanced workflows included orchestrating device provisioning, monitoring cloud resources, and building resilient, automatic services for network self-healing and compliance. Every step in this chapter focused upon scalable automation, allowing us to bridge traditional networks, cloud platforms, and business applications through reliable, well-structured code.

Chapter 8: Network Programming with AsyncIO

Chapter Overview

In this chapter, we will discover why asynchronous programming is quickly becoming essential for network engineers and automation professionals who need to scale operations beyond small scripts or manual workflows. We will start by exploring the real-world challenges of managing hundreds of devices, APIs, or event streams, and learn why synchronous programming models can no longer keep up.

As the chapter progresses, we will be introduced to the foundational ideas behind asynchronous code, then dive deep into Python's **`asyncio`** library, the event loop, coroutines, and tasks, breaking down how each part works and how we can leverage them in the own automation projects. Through detailed, live-coding examples, we will learn to launch parallel API calls, handle asynchronous file operations, and robustly manage errors or network delays. We will see how async workflows differ from traditional approaches, when to use them for maximum effect, and how they pair with other tools for cloud and on-premises network automation. By the end, we will be equipped to build scalable, resource-efficient automation scripts that keep pace with today's ever-growing network demands.

Introducing Asynchronous Programming

Need for Async

These days, network environments are always on the go. We're handling more and more devices every day, automating more and more processes, and integrating with cloud services, APIs, and analytics platforms. In this landscape, waiting is everywhere: we wait for devices to respond, for configuration changes to be acknowledged, or for bulk monitoring data to arrive. In traditional (synchronous) code, the script or tool pauses for each response before moving on to the next device or task. But when we scale up and work with hundreds or thousands of endpoints, these pauses add up. That makes the automation slow, inefficient, and resource-hungry.

That's where asynchronous programming comes in. Instead of making the code wait, we can run multiple operations at the same time. We can move on to the next task as soon as we're done with the current one. This means we can talk to hundreds of devices, poll dozens of APIs, or handle a flood of incoming events, all at once, without slowing down the process. In the world of network engineering, async programming isn't just about "faster math" — it's about supercharging multitasking. Imagine a script that can handle a ton of jobs, whether they're slow or network-dependent, all at once.

Synchronous vs. Asynchronous Workflows

To clear up any confusion, I'll use an example. Let's say we're at a busy coffee shop. In a synchronous model, the barista takes one order at a time, waits for the customer to pay, prepares the drink, delivers it, and then starts the next order. It works well when business is slow, but when there's a long line, customers have to wait, and the barista's time is wasted whenever someone fumble for cash or ask questions. In an asynchronous workflow, the barista might take several orders in a row, start each drink, and call out names as each one is ready. Your customers get served faster, and the barista doesn't have to wait around as long. In networking and automation, async lets the scripts act like a super efficient barista, handling a ton of operations at once, maximizing throughput, and minimizing wasted cycles.

Real Benefits for Network Engineers

The async programming is especially valuable for any task where waiting for I/O, network requests, file reads, API calls, database queries, is the main bottleneck. We see this in network polling, cloud management, device onboarding, or event-driven monitoring. By adopting async, we can:

- Dramatically reduce the total time for large jobs, since we are not stuck waiting for slow devices or services.
- Lower resource usage, because a single process can manage many jobs in parallel, no need to launch dozens of threads or processes.
- Build more responsive, scalable automation that can handle bursts of activity or sudden spikes in workload.

When we work with large-scale network automation, async programming isn't just a "nice-to-have", it's often the only practical way to meet real-world requirements for speed, reliability, and efficiency. We will use this in situations like:

- Polling hundreds of devices for status updates.
- Orchestrating batch changes across many endpoints.
- Aggregating data from multiple APIs in parallel.
- Handling events or messages in real-time from network sensors, logs, or security alerts.

Further, we will see exactly how Python implements async (with **`asyncio`** and other libraries), how to write the own async routines, and how to use them to maximize the power and responsiveness of the network automation scripts.

AsyncIO Library

What Is AsyncIO?

Once we understand the need for asynchronous programming, Python's **`asyncio`** library becomes the main tool for building efficient, scalable, and responsive network automation. **`asyncio`** brings an event-driven programming model to Python, allowing us to launch and manage multiple I/O-bound operations concurrently within a single process. We can use

asyncio to schedule, pause, and resume dozens or hundreds of network requests, all without the overhead of threads or the complexity of external frameworks. This is particularly valuable in real-world scenarios where the code needs to communicate with many devices, APIs, or services at the same time. With **asyncio**, the script "waits" for I/O in a non-blocking way, using coroutines and an event loop, making the most of every second and every CPU cycle.

Event Loops and Coroutines

At the core of **asyncio** are ***event loops*** and ***coroutines***. An event loop acts as the conductor, managing and scheduling tasks that are ready to run. Coroutines are the musicians, functions we define with **async def** that can pause their work with **await** while waiting for I/O, allowing other coroutines to use the event loop in the meantime. This means that we don't need to create threads or processes to get concurrency; we simply launch coroutines, and Python does the rest. We start the event loop with **asyncio.run(main())**, where **main** is an **async def** function that kicks off the automation tasks.

Running Coroutines

Let us try to skill it with a situation wherein we want to ping several hosts or make multiple HTTP requests at once. So here, we need to define a coroutine for each operation, then schedule them together. The following script is how we would launch multiple jobs in parallel using **asyncio.create_task** and **await**:

```
import asyncio
async def poll_device(host):
    print(f"Connecting to {host}...")
    await asyncio.sleep(1)  # Simulating network delay
    print(f"Completed check for {host}")
async def main():
    hosts = ["switch01", "router02", "firewall03"]
    tasks = [asyncio.create_task(poll_device(host)) for host
in hosts]
    await asyncio.gather(*tasks)
asyncio.run(main())
```

In the above, all the device polls start immediately, and each one completes as soon as its work is done. The code never blocks unnecessarily, so the scripts finish far faster than if we waited for each device in turn.

Awaitables, Tasks, and Scheduling

The **asyncio** builds on the concept of awaitables, objects we can **await** on, such as coroutines, tasks, or even asynchronous generators. When we schedule a coroutine as a task (**asyncio.create_task( )**), it's registered with the event loop and runs independently. If the script needs to kick off hundreds of background jobs, say, polling interface stats from every switch in a large network, we can schedule them all at once. The event loop ensures that every time a coroutine is paused (for I/O), another one gets a chance to run. This allows a single process to handle massive concurrency, limited only by system resources and network bandwidth.

Integrating AsyncIO

Many of the modern network and today's most of the web libraries are now built with async support. Some of the popular libraries such as **aiohttp** (for HTTP), **aiomysql** (for MySQL databases), and **asyncssh** (for SSH connections) gives us a total advantage of Python's event-driven capabilities to launch dozens of jobs at once and handle responses as they arrive. So for example, if we want to retrieve status from 100 APIs, fetch thousands of log lines, or push updates across an entire device fleet, the **asyncio** makes these operations fast, reliable, and maintainable. The more we work with **asyncio**, the more we will appreciate the power and flexibility it brings to network automation and I/O-heavy applications.

AsyncIO for IO Bound Operations

AsyncIO for IO-Bound

Most of the time, when we use network automation, the scripts are waiting for network devices, databases, files, or APIs to respond, not for CPU. These are classic IO-bound scenarios. But in a synchronous world, the code would block on each operation: sending a command to a switch, querying a cloud API, writing to disk, or fetching results from a database. It's like we're flipping the script, so each time the script would "wait," it gives control to another task. The result is powerful concurrency, using one event loop and process, with zero wasted time.

And AsyncIO is the tool that makes this not just possible, but natural and scalable. It can poll hundreds of devices, scrape dozens of APIs, or serve thousands of clients, all at once and all from a single Python process. And the benefits are immediate: automation jobs finish faster, we use fewer resources, and we gain new ways to orchestrate complex workflows across a modern network.

AsyncIO for Parallel API Requests

Let us learn it practically for a situation like wherein we want to gather interface status from 100 switches, each exposing a REST API. So here, instead of querying them one at a time, AsyncIO allows us launch every request at once and process replies as they arrive. Following is how we would do it with **aiohttp**, the async HTTP library for Python.

At first, we will install **aiohttp**:

```
pip install aiohttp
```

Now, we then perform the Async polling of multiple devices, as below:

```
import asyncio
import aiohttp
device_urls = [f"https://api.switches.local/device/{i}/status"
for i in range(1, 101)]
AUTH_TOKEN = "YOUR_API_TOKEN"
async def fetch_status(session, url):
    headers = {"Authorization": f"Bearer {AUTH_TOKEN}"}
    async with session.get(url, headers=headers) as response:
        if response.status == 200:
            data = await response.json()
            print(f"{url}: {data['status']}")
            return data
        else:
            print(f"{url}: Failed ({response.status})")
            return None
async def main():
    async with aiohttp.ClientSession() as session:
        tasks = [fetch_status(session, url) for url in
device_urls]
        results = await asyncio.gather(*tasks)
asyncio.run(main())
```

Here, every status check starts nearly instantly. The AsyncIO manages the waiting and concurrency for you. We can scale this pattern to thousands of requests if needed, limited only by bandwidth and system resources.

Handling IO-Bound Tasks

Async File Operations

While Python's standard file IO is not natively async, third-party libraries like **aiofiles** fill the gap for disk-bound automation:

```
pip install aiofiles
import aiofiles
import asyncio
async def write_log(filename, message):
    async with aiofiles.open(filename, 'a') as f:
        await f.write(message + '\n')
async def main():
    await write_log('automation.log', 'Task started')
    await write_log('automation.log', 'Task completed')
asyncio.run(main())
```

This approach allows us log or process files in parallel with other tasks, ideal for high-throughput automation pipelines.

Async Database Operations

Libraries like **aiomysql** and **aiopg** (Postgres) bring the same efficiency to database interactions. For example, we might store device health data in a SQL database, handling thousands of records per minute without blocking the script.

Async Socket Operations

For lower-level tasks, such as custom protocols, scanning, or monitoring, we can use **asyncio**'s built-in networking. We can open hundreds of sockets, serve thousands of clients, or aggregate data streams without threading headaches.

Error Handling and Throttling

AsyncIO offers amazing speed, but we have to be careful with error handling and rate limiting, especially when working with network APIs or fragile devices. It's always a good idea to wrap async tasks in try/except blocks, log any failures, and implement back-off or retry logic for APIs that rate-limit or drop connections.

Following a small but an interesting sample program to perform robust error handling:

```
async def fetch_status(session, url):
    try:
        headers = {"Authorization": f"Bearer {AUTH_TOKEN}"}
        async with session.get(url, headers=headers,
timeout=10) as response:
            if response.status == 200:
                data = await response.json()
                print(f"{url}: {data['status']}")
                return data
            else:
                print(f"{url}: Failed ({response.status})")
                return None
    except asyncio.TimeoutError:
        print(f"{url}: Timed out")
    except Exception as e:
        print(f"{url}: Error - {e}")
```

in the above, we can throttle requests using **`asyncio.Semaphore`** if APIs or devices cannot handle unlimited concurrency. The AsyncIO is best used when the script waits for responses from:

- REST or SOAP APIs (network devices, cloud services, monitoring tools)
- SSH, Telnet, or proprietary network sockets (with async libraries)
- File IO (especially for log aggregation or parallel data processing)
- Databases (with async drivers)
- Message queues and event-driven workflows

If the task is CPU-bound (cryptography, data crunching, image processing), the async will not help, but it shines for everything that involves network or IO waits.

Summary

Throughout this chapter, we learned how asynchronous programming transforms the way network automation handles large-scale, IO-bound operations. We began by understanding why traditional, synchronous scripts fall short when faced with many devices or cloud services that respond at different speeds. The concept of asynchronous programming was demystified, showing how it allows the code to manage multiple operations at once without unnecessary waiting. We then explored the **asyncio** library, mastering its event loop, coroutines, and task scheduling, and saw how to structure Python code so that dozens or hundreds of network calls, file writes, or log events can be managed efficiently.

There are real-world scenarios illustrated, and it shows the difference async makes in device polling, API aggregation, file logging, and more. We reviewed practical scripts for parallel API requests, asynchronous file writes, and robust error handling, ensuring the automation is not just fast but also reliable under high load. Finally, we learned to identify when async programming is best suited, especially for network and IO-heavy jobs, enabling the scripts to finish faster, consume fewer resources, and handle scale without complexity. Each concept was supported by practical, ready-to-use patterns for modern network engineering.

CHAPTER 9: NETWORK TESTING AND SIMULATION

Chapter Overview

This chapter's going to teach we how network testing and simulation are key to reliable and scalable infrastructure management. First, we will learn why testing is important, and we will see all kinds of ways to test, from basic health checks to really intense, long-term reliability tests and capacity and error analysis. We will get hands-on with Python-powered tools like ping3, iperf3, and Locust, learning how to measure, monitor, and benchmark everything from latency and jitter to peak bandwidth and failure rates.

This chapter will walk we through the real-world practices for designing effective tests, analyzing results, and using the findings to drive smarter, safer change across the environment. We'll also introduce us to SimPy, a simulation framework that allows us experiment with topologies, policies, and "what-if" scenarios. This helps we predict outcomes and avoid costly surprises. By the time we are done with this chapter, we will be ready to move past the guesswork. We will be using data-driven insights and practical automation to build, validate, and continuously improve the networks, whatever the future holds.

Introduction to Network Testing and Simulation

Central to IT Services

Every modern network, whether local or global, simple or hybrid-cloud, faces relentless change, new applications, rising user loads, evolving security threats, and shifting topologies. For networks to remain reliable, secure, and high performing, we need to do more than just react to issues as they arise. We must proactively test, measure, and simulate its behavior under a range of real-world and hypothetical conditions. This is the only way to ensure new deployments don't introduce bottlenecks, that upgrades won't break existing workflows, and that the infrastructure is truly ready for peak demand, disaster scenarios, or the next big business pivot.

The concept of network testing and simulation go hand in hand. The testing tells us how the network performs ***right now***, under actual load, with real users and devices, exposing live vulnerabilities, and measuring end-to-end metrics like latency, throughput, jitter, and error rates. The simulation allows us safely predict ***what will happen*** in situations that are risky, impractical, or expensive to test in production, such as a major outage, a DDoS attack, or a sudden doubling of user demand. If we combine altogether, it wil give us the ability to prevent issues before they hit, optimize investments, and prove compliance with business and regulatory goals.

What We Test, Measure, and Simulate?

The function of network testing encompasses several intertwined methodologies:

- ***Performance Testing*** measures raw speed (throughput), responsiveness (latency), stability under fluctuating load (jitter), and reliability (packet loss). We will want to see not just average metrics, but how performance shifts as the network is stressed with many users or heavy traffic.
- ***Reliability Testing*** probes the network's ability to operate without interruption over time, even as devices fail, links go down, or workloads spike unexpectedly. Can the core services recover gracefully, or does one error cascade into a larger outage?
- ***Capacity Testing*** determines the absolute limit of the network's infrastructure. At what point do switches, firewalls, wireless access points, or Internet uplinks begin to drop packets, slow down, or fail outright? Knowing the "breaking point" allows us plan upgrades before users are affected.
- ***Security Testing*** examines the defenses, can we identify and block malicious activity, withstand common attacks, or detect misconfigurations that expose sensitive data? Security testing ranges from simple port scans to full-scale penetration testing, both manual and automated. And,
- ***Simulation*** that goes beyond passive measurement. Here, we construct models of the network and simulate traffic patterns, failures, new device deployments, or topology changes in a controlled, risk-free environment. We can experiment with upgrades, congestion controls, or routing changes before touching the live network.

Python Toolkit

As always, the Python stands out as the go-to language for modern network testing and simulation. It's got three big advantages: rich libraries, cross-platform compatibility, and a massive community that's always coming up with new tools and patterns. Rather than being stuck with a proprietary GUI, we use scripts, automation, and a combination of tests as needed. The results go into dashboards, we integrate with CI/CD pipelines, or we run complex simulation scenarios. With Python, we can quickly switch between testing production hardware, simulating network models, analyzing logs, or building custom visualizations. Sometimes, all of these can be done in just one script!

We'll be using these Python libraries:

- ***ping3:*** For low-level, programmatic ping tests, measuring basic connectivity and latency.
- ***iperf3-python:*** For active bandwidth measurement and throughput testing.
- ***Locust:*** For high-level, user-centric load and reliability testing, simulating real-world usage patterns.
- ***Scapy:*** For deep, custom packet crafting, protocol analysis, and security probing.
- ***SimPy:*** For full-featured network simulations, including modeling complex topologies, dynamic traffic, and resource contention.
- ***NetworkX:*** For analyzing network graphs and understanding large-scale connectivity or failure scenarios.

All these tools facilitate to automate everything from nightly health checks to one-off stress tests or simulation experiments. Instead of running a few CLI tools by hand, we build pipelines and repeatable routines, catching problems early, testing hypotheses, and validating fixes before they're rolled out.

Popular Network Testing Methodologies

Every time we start a network test, we should take a step back and clarify what we want to learn about the environment. When it comes to network testing, there's more to it than just running commands or collecting numbers. It's a methodical approach that makes sure the results are reliable, repeatable, and actually helpful in addressing the business's real-world issues. Testing isn't a one-size-fits-all thing. What works for a new fiber link might not work for a WiFi upgrade, DDoS risk assessment, or failover plan. It's all about picking the right methodology for the scenario and sticking to it so we can compare results across time, sites, or device types. Having this mindset also helps us communicate results to leadership, justify investments, and defend the network design with data rather than guesswork.

Connectivity Testing

Every network starts with a simple question: "**Can these devices communicate**?" the connectivity testing forms the baseline for every other methodology, verifying that routing, cabling, firewall rules, and physical connections all align. While a simple ping is often enough for initial verification, true connectivity testing can include ARP resolution, DNS lookups, TCP/UDP port checks, and even "synthetic" user actions (like a script that signs in to a web app). For critical paths, we may script ongoing connectivity probes with Python, logging the results and sending alerts if devices drop out of reach. Good connectivity methodology involves not just initial "green light" checks, but long-term monitoring for flapping links, intermittent failures, or service outages. It allowed to build historical baselines and catch trends before users complain.

Latency and Jitter Measurement

Once we confirm basic connectivity, the next challenge is measuring ***how well*** the devices communicate. Latency is the round-trip time for data between endpoints, while jitter tracks the variation in those times, both are critical for voice, video, or real-time services. The methodologies here involve sustained ping tests, traceroutes to spot routing changes, and dedicated tools to log latency at various times of day or under different loads. Also, the high or variable latency often reveals hidden problems: overloaded links, routing loops, misconfigured QoS, or wireless interference. The methodology should include regular, automated measurement to multiple destinations, analysis of trends over time, and integration with change management, so we can correlate spikes with recent upgrades, config changes, or known incidents. In fact, the Jitter measurement, in particular, is vital for validating WAN and internet circuits used for VoIP or conferencing.

Bandwidth and Throughput Testing

Knowing the network "works" is not enough if it can't handle business demand. Throughput and bandwidth testing reveal the infrastructure's ability to move data at speed, exposing congestion, misconfigured QoS, or hardware bottlenecks. There are effective methodologies that make use of active tools like ***iperf3*** to send controlled data streams between endpoints, measuring both upload and download rates, packet loss, and even CPU utilization on test devices. For wireless and cloud environments, combine multiple locations, times, and traffic mixes to get a realistic view. In production, we can think of both "clean" tests (with no other traffic) and "realistic" ones (during peak hours).

Load, Stress, and Soak Testing

The networks are designed for peaks, not just averages. The load testing simulates normal business activity, hundreds of users logging in, opening documents, making calls, while stress testing pushes the environment to its limits. And, the soak testing goes further, running these loads for hours or days to expose memory leaks, hardware overheating, or unexpected state changes. It is advisable to make use of tools like ***Locust***, custom Python scripts, or dedicated appliances to generate realistic traffic patterns. We will want to vary the number of simulated users, transaction types, and timing, as well as inject background noise (like backup jobs or cloud sync). After each test, analyze device logs, interface stats, and error counters to see how systems held up. There are good methodologies that includes "ramp up" and "ramp down" phases, recovery testing, and full documentation of the traffic models.

Packet Loss and Error Rate Testing

We're not really getting anything out of a network that only works "most of the time." The way we test for packet loss and error rate is by digging into the details and looking for dropped packets, retransmits, corrupted frames, or high error counters on switch/router interfaces. You can start with ICMP or UDP flood tests, but if you want to go even deeper, try using protocol-aware tools like TCP-based iperf3 tests or synthetic application probes. When it comes to wireless or WAN, try combining packet capture with event correlation. Do errors happen more often when it rains, when doors open, or when specific devices join the network? And always script repeated tests over time and correlate them with device logs, syslogs, or SNMP traps. A good method isn't just about pointing out "bad" numbers; it connects them to their root causes. Those causes might be cabling, firmware, interference, or environmental factors.

Security, Vulnerability, and Compliance Testing

The point is, security testing is its own special skill, but the way you do it is very important. For starters, you have to keep your eye out for open ports, run scans for weak spots, make sure access control lists and firewalls are up to snuff, and make sure you're doing things by the book with standards like PCI or ISO 27001. A solid methodology separates routine scanning from targeted penetration testing, keeps test tools up to date, and documents every step for audit. You can also include the tests in change management, scanning before and after changes to catch any regressions. We can script to automate reporting, and then combine the results with your incident response plan so you can quickly react to threats.

Simulation and Modeling

Finally, the simulation is one that goes where testing cannot. We can use SimPy or virtual lab platforms (like GNS3, EVE-NG, or vendor sandboxes) to model changes, test failovers, or predict growth. We can strongly adopt the methdologhy here focusing on realism: **use accurate topologies, realistic traffic profiles, and model both normal operations and edge cases**. What we need to do is to simulate the impact of a new site, additional users, or vendor change before touching production. When combined with real test data, our simulation will allows us to "see the future" and make decisions with confidence.

Performance Testing using ping3 and iperf3

The Python's popularity in network automation means we can embed real, production-grade testing directly into the scripts, dashboards, and CI/CD pipelines. The Python does have ***ping3*** and ***iperf3*** as its two standout libraries, which are capable of measuring the "real" performance of the network.

Measuring Latency and Packet Loss

The **`ping3`** library is a pure Python alternative to the classic ping command. It allows us script and automate ICMP echo requests, perfect for connectivity checks, latency stats, and basic network monitoring.

To begin with, we get the library on board:

```
pip install ping3
```

And, now we create a script for a simple ping test as below:

```
from ping3 import ping, verbose_ping
# Quick single ping
response = ping("8.8.8.8")
if response is not None:
    print(f"Ping successful! Round-trip time:
{response*1000:.2f} ms")
else:
```

```
    print("Ping failed.")
# Multiple pings with stats
verbose_ping("1.1.1.1", count=5)
```

We can also expand this script to loop over subnets, monitor latency to all branches, or even trigger alerts if average RTT or packet loss exceeds thresholds.

For example, let us take another example wherein we can test for a list of devices, as shown below:

```
devices = ["8.8.8.8", "1.1.1.1", "192.168.1.1"]
results = {}
for host in devices:
    rtt = ping(host, timeout=2)
    results[host] = rtt if rtt else "timeout"
print(results)
```

As for production scripts, you should always handle exceptions. Keep in mind that hosts may block ICMP, so we'll need to detect and log timeouts or permission errors.

Bandwidth and Throughput Testing

The ***iperf3*** is the industry standard for active bandwidth measurement between two endpoints. The Python wrapper, ***iperf3-python***, allows us automate and parse these tests directly from the code.

To begin with, we will first install the iperf3 on both endpoints:

```
sudo apt install iperf3
pip install iperf3
```

to carry out the testing, we start with an iperf3 server on one device:

```
iperf3 -s
```

From the Python script (on the client side):

```
import iperf3
client = iperf3.Client()
client.server_hostname = '192.168.1.10'  # iperf3 server IP
client.port = 5201  # default iperf3 port
```

```
client.duration = 10  # seconds
result = client.run()
if result.error:
    print(f"Error: {result.error}")
else:
    print(f"Sent: {result.sent_Mbps} Mbps")
    print(f"Received: {result.received_Mbps} Mbps")
    print(f"Jitter: {getattr(result, 'jitter_ms', 'n/a')} ms")
```

This code will initiate a 10-second bandwidth test, print both upload and download rates, and, if applicable, the jitter measurement for UDP streams. We can also wrap the above in loops to test many paths, compare wired vs wireless performance, or build automated daily/weekly benchmarks for trend analysis.

Reliability Testing using Locust

Exploring Locust

The Locust is a powerful, Python-based load-testing tool built to simulate real user activity against the networks, APIs, or services. Unlike legacy stress testers, this tool allows us script complex behaviors in Python, scale tests across distributed worker nodes, and visualize results in real time. In fact, what makes Locust special for network engineers and SREs is its blend of flexibility and scalability: we can simulate anything from simple HTTP API calls to full authentication workflows, DNS lookups, or device provisioning routines, then push these tests to thousands or even millions of virtual "users."

The Locust excels at two vital forms of network testing:

- ***Reliability testing***, which looks for failures, flapping, or error spikes over time.
- ***Capacity testing***, which reveals the maximum sustainable load the system can handle before errors, slowdowns, or resource exhaustion.

Configuring Locust

So, at first, we will set up Locust right into our Python environment via pip:

```
pip install locust
locust --version
```

Now, we can proceed to define the load test scenarios as Python scripts.

Demystifying Reliability Testing

The concept of reliability testing is not about proving the network or service can handle a huge spike for a few minutes, it's about confirming that it can stay healthy, responsive, and error-free during the steady, everyday churn of real user activity. When we run reliability tests, the goal is to simulate the "heartbeat" of the organization: hundreds or thousands of devices, users, or automated jobs sending regular requests, reading and writing data, or polling APIs hour after hour. The key aim of carrying out the reliability testing is to uncover subtle issues, memory leaks, state drift, slow performance, or sporadic failures, that only surface over extended, steady use. So, without reliability testing, we risk shipping services or automation routines that work for a demo but collapse after days of actual use.

Scripting Reliability Test

Now to learn reliability test, we'll focus upon the mimicking of the normal daily operations. And this could be like polling a device API every few seconds, logging in and out of a dashboard, or fetching health stats from a switch.

So, I have prepared a script to test for a REST API endpoint that serves device status:

```
from locust import HttpUser, task, between
class DeviceHealthCheckUser(HttpUser):
    wait_time = between(2, 10)  # Simulate normal polling
intervals
    @task
    def poll_health(self):
        response = self.client.get("/api/device/health")
        if response.status_code == 200:
            # Optionally verify content or parse JSON here
            pass
        else:
            print(f"Failure: {response.status_code}")
```

We then run the above script with:

```
locust -f locustfile.py --host http://your-api-server.local
```

and then we open **http://localhost:8089** to start hundreds or thousands of simulated users, each behaving like a monitoring agent.

Analyze Reliability Test Results

When we do these tests, we're looking for trends, not just whether it worked, but whether it worked every time, for every user, over hours or days. If you can, run the test for several hours to see how it holds up. While the test is running, Locust gives us live dashboards and detailed CSV output (using --csv).

We need to be on the lookout for:

- Gradual increases in response time (memory leaks or resource contention).
- Fluctuations in error rates (occasional API hiccups, not just hard failures).
- Any recurring failures at specific intervals (possible scheduled jobs, backups, or external dependencies).

And you can use the Locust data to check the system and network logs, CPU, memory, and bandwidth metrics to see what caused a dip in performance or an error spike. You can always count on something if it passes the test — no matter what.

Capacity Testing using Locust

The concept of capacity testing asks a simple but vital question: ***How much traffic, how many users, or how many operations can my service handle before performance degrades or errors begin to appear?*** Unlike reliability testing, which holds load steady, the capacity testing ramps it up, sometimes gently, sometimes aggressively, until we hit a breaking point. This isn't just about proving peak numbers to stakeholders; it's about revealing where the bottlenecks are, when queueing or backpressure begins, and how gracefully the system copes with overload.

Now, to perform a capacity test, we can use the same Locust setup done previously but now we will focus on ramping up the number of users. In the Locust web UI, we will set a high user target and a spawn rate to increase load over time. Alternatively, we can make use of headless mode for scripted, repeatable runs as below:

```
locust -f locustfile.py --host http://your-api-server.local --
users 5000 --spawn-rate 100 --headless --run-time 20m --csv
cap_test
```

With this, it launches 5,000 simulated users, adding 100 per second, and runs for 20 minutes. The Locust tracks request rate, failures, and latency throughout.

Now we do also know that the capacity testing is about the curve, and it is not a single number. So here, we must also watch for:

- Where response times begin to rise sharply ("knee point").
- When failures (timeouts, 5xx errors) start to spike.
- If error rates climb before or after CPU/network exhaustion.

After this, we can then use the exported CSVs for post-test analysis and plotting. Apart from this, we can then plan for horizontal scaling, hardware upgrades, or code optimization.

Network Simulation with Simpy

When we face questions that real-world testing can't answer, such as "What if my network topology changes?" or "How would my system behave during a partial outage or a sudden traffic spike?", simulation becomes the most valuable tool. The ***SimPy*** is a process-based discrete-event simulation framework written in Python. It allows us model and analyze the behavior of complex systems by representing devices, links, users, or queues as code objects that interact over time, following real or hypothetical rules.

The SimPy is ideal for network professionals because it balances power and simplicity. Unlike vendor-specific emulators or heavyweight modeling suites, SimPy is lightweight, scriptable, and integrates easily with the Python automation workflows. We can use it to:

- Prototype new architectures or routing policies before making costly changes.
- Understand queueing, congestion, or failover behavior under controlled, repeatable conditions. And,
- Run "what-if" analyses on device failure, load variation, or policy changes, without any risk to production.

Installing SimPy

We can add and verify the SimPy inside our Python virtual environment:

```
pip install simpy
import simpy
print(simpy.__version__)
```

And, then we are ready to build network simulations alongside any other Python automation tasks.

Building a Simple Network Queue Simulation

The SimPy allows us represent the components of the network as "processes" that interact using events, think routers, switches, links, and packets as code objects. We can simulate traffic arrival, transmission delays, queueing, link failures, or resource contention. The key is that SimPy models time explicitly, so we can observe not just what happens, but when, making it perfect for studying performance under different scenarios.

Let us take an example of modeling a simple network queue, with simulating a scenario where devices send packets to a router that processes them one at a time.

```
import simpy
import random
def packet_generator(env, router, arrival_rate):
    packet_id = 0
    while True:
        yield env.timeout(random.expovariate(arrival_rate))  #
Random arrival interval
        packet_id += 1
        env.process(packet_router(env, router, packet_id))
def packet_router(env, router, packet_id):
    arrival_time = env.now
    with router.request() as req:
        yield req
        yield env.timeout(2)  # Processing time per packet (in
seconds)
        print(f"Packet {packet_id} processed at time
{env.now:.2f}, waited {env.now - arrival_time:.2f} seconds.")
env = simpy.Environment()
router = simpy.Resource(env, capacity=1)  # 1 = single router,
single queue
# Start generator with average arrival rate (e.g., 0.5
packets/sec)
env.process(packet_generator(env, router, arrival_rate=0.5))
env.run(until=20)
```

In the above, the script actually simulates the packet arrivals at random intervals, each being queued at the router. The simulation then prints when each packet is processed and how long it waited, giving insight into queue build-up, processing delays, and resource utilization.

In addition, we can add more complexity, such as:

- Multiple routers or links (for mesh or star topologies).

- Variable processing times or link speeds.
- Simulating packet drops if queues fill up.
- Modeling failures and automatic failover.
- Collecting statistics over hundreds or thousands of events for analysis.

Adding Parallel Simulation

We can also have multiple devices getting simulated parallely. And for this, we simply add a second router in parallel as shown in the below:

```
router1 = simpy.Resource(env, capacity=1)
router2 = simpy.Resource(env, capacity=1)
# Distribute packets to router1 or router2 based on custom
logic
```

In the above, we might also simulate traffic from different device types (IoT sensors, user workstations, video streams) with different arrival rates and priorities. The SimPy empowers us to "test the future" before it arrives, saving costs, avoiding downtime, and making smart, data-driven choices about upgrades, redundancy, or policy.

Summary

Throughout this chapter, we learned how testing and simulation are foundational to building reliable, high-performing, and resilient networks. We learned how modern network testing is not limited to pinging devices but spans a wide range of methodologies, including connectivity checks, latency and jitter measurement, throughput and bandwidth validation, stress and soak tests, error and loss detection, and vulnerability assessments. We gained practical, step-by-step experience using Python-powered tools like ping3 for latency and loss analysis, iperf3 for bandwidth and performance benchmarking, and Locust for orchestrating large-scale reliability and capacity tests that mimic real-world usage and uncover subtle, long-term issues.

We discovered how carefully designed testing can reveal not just outages but patterns of degradation, scaling limits, or the hidden impact of daily business activity. The chapter also introduced SimPy, showing how simulation allows us model the future, analyze topologies, and experiment with changes or failures in a risk-free environment. Each technique was tied back to its business value, enabling proactive planning, proof of compliance, informed upgrades, and a deep confidence in the infrastructure's ability to evolve and withstand change.

CHAPTER 10: NETWORK CONFIGURATION MANAGEMENT

Chapter Overview

This chapter is all about to develop skillset that builds the capability to bring true order, safety, and agility to network configuration management in any environment, whether enterprise, service provider, or cloud-based. We will discover the essential role that version control, backup, and configuration management tools play in delivering secure, stable, and compliant network operations. The chapter will introduce us to powerful automation libraries like NAPALM and orchestration frameworks such as Nornir, helping we connect, audit, and control devices at scale.

As we progress, we will explore how to automate every step of the configuration lifecycle, from routine backups to rapid restores, and how to roll out changes across dozens or hundreds of devices with minimal risk. We will see how advanced orchestration, event-driven automation, and CI/CD-style pipelines transform manual tasks into seamless, auditable processes that match the pace of business change. By the end of this chapter, we will be equipped to design, implement, and maintain network configuration workflows that are robust, compliant, and fully ready for tomorrow's demands, so we can manage even the most complex environments with confidence and clarity.

Network Configuration Management (NCM)

Why NCM Matters?

Every solid, secure, and flexible network depends on accurate and traceable setup. NCM is all about keeping an eye on the network settings and making sure that the only changes that go live are the ones we intended. It also gives us the power to audit, roll back, and automate the network — and all at scale! When we step into any real enterprise, whether it's a campus, data center, or hybrid cloud, the network is like a living organism. It's got switches, routers, firewalls, and edge appliances constantly updating routes, rules, and policies. If we accidentally misconfigure something, miss a backup, or make an undocumented change, we could end up with outages, security vulnerabilities, or hours of firefighting. NCM is all about turning chaos into order, making sure that every device's configuration is intentional, recoverable and in line with the business requirements. As networks get bigger and more complex, it's no longer possible to do manual configuration by CLI. The way forward is versioning, automation, and policy-driven management.

NCM Core Objectives

NCM work is all about visibility, consistency, auditability, and control. We need to know what's running on every device, who changed what, and the time and cause of any service interruptions so we can restore it right away. The best NCM processes have a tight feedback loop: capture configs, validate them, back them up, compare against known-good baselines, and automate as much as possible. And at the heart of this workflow is version control. If we keep every configuration snapshot in a version-controlled system like Git, we will have a time machine for the network. That way, we can review changes, revert bad pushes, prove compliance, and pass audits. We won't have to guess or sift through old emails or manual notes. It's like the insurance policy. If we automate regular pulls of device configs and store them both locally and remotely, we will have a rapid path to recovery even if a device fails or gets wiped.

Modern NCM Toolbox

The landscape of NCM tools has evolved quickly. We've gone from proprietary, platform-specific appliances to flexible, Python-driven frameworks and open-source platforms. Following are the main categories and what they offer:

- ***Open-Source Python Libraries*** like ***NAPALM*** (Network Automation and Programmability Abstraction Layer with Multivendor support) and ***Netmiko*** allows us to connect, retrieve, compare, and push configurations across a wide mix of vendor devices. With a consistent API, we can script backups, automate merges, or roll back configs without ever touching the CLI.
- ***Vendor Platforms*** such as Cisco Prime Infrastructure, Junos Space, or Aruba AirWave provide rich dashboards and automated workflows, but may lock we into a single vendor ecosystem. For multi-vendor or brownfield environments, open libraries or platform-agnostic NMS solutions are often preferred.
- ***Network Management Systems*** like SolarWinds NCM, RANCID, or Oxidized focus on pulling configs, tracking changes, and generating alerts on drift or unauthorized edits. These often pair with open-source or cloud-based version control for complete change tracking.
- ***Configuration-as-Code and GitOps*** are mush in use. Increasingly. Organizations are grtadually storing configs in Git repositories, using automation to push intended state to devices (similar to DevOps practices for software). This allows us build approval workflows, validate changes before deployment, and instantly roll back to a last-known-good config if issues arise.

In today's time, a modern NCM stack often combines a hybrid approach, like the scripting with Python for flexibility, the NMS for monitoring and alerting, and the Git for authoritative version control and auditability.

Automating Configuration Management with Python

The true power of modern NCM is realized when we automate every step, from config retrieval, to validation, to deployment. The python library like NAPALM can give us a consistent, vendor-agnostic interface for connecting to devices, regardless of whether we are working with Cisco, Juniper, Arista, or other major platforms.

The automation of the config management will allows us to:

- Schedule regular config pulls and backups without manual intervention.
- Generate alerts if unauthorized or accidental changes are detected.

- Test and validate configs for syntax or policy errors before pushing them live. And,
- Batch-update device settings, VLANs, ACLs, or routing tables, reducing human error and speeding up network changes.

Following is a sample program on the automation:

To begin, we first get the **napalm** installed as below:

```
pip install napalm gitpython
```

Then, we create a script to retrieve and version-control configs:

```
import napalm
from git import Repo
import os
from datetime import datetime
def backup_and_commit(host, user, pwd, driver, repo_path):
    napalm_driver = napalm.get_network_driver(driver)
    with napalm_driver(host, user, pwd) as device:
        config = device.get_config()['running']
        filename =
f"{repo_path}/{host}_config_{datetime.now().strftime('%Y%m%d_%
H%M%S')}.txt"
        with open(filename, 'w') as f:
            f.write(config)
        repo = Repo(repo_path)
        repo.git.add(filename)
        repo.git.commit('-m', f"Backup config from {host} at
{datetime.now().isoformat()}")
backup_and_commit('10.0.0.1', 'admin', 'password', 'ios',
'/path/to/your/repo')
```

We can also adapt this to pull from every device in the fleet, or automate the process via cron, and then push the results to our secure Git remote.

However, with automation, we must not forget to ensure the following tips:

- Don't forget to test scripts in a lab or non-production environment before use.

- Do not forget to carry out the robust error handling, log failed backups, retries, and authentication errors.
- Do not forget to secure the credentials.
- Just confirm that we have validated the configs for policy and the syntaxes before pushing them live.
- And, finally, make use of the dry-run or "compare" modes to preview changes before actual deployment.

NAPALM for Version Control and Backup

The management of modern, multi-vendor networks, brings a landscape that is filled with switches, routers, and firewalls from Cisco, Juniper, Arista, Huawei, and more. Now, each device comes with its own command-line quirks, API formats, and configuration approaches. So here, keeping the configs synchronized, changes tracked, and compliance assured is like creating endless custom scripts and vendor lock-in. The development of ***NAPALM (Network Automation and Programmability Abstraction Layer with Multivendor support)*** was meant to break that cycle.

This NAPALM thing gives us one interface to work with lots of different hardware platforms. We can use it to work with any vendor, so the code stays the same no matter what. NAPALM is great for handling connectivity, authentication, config retrieval, comparison, pushing, and rollback, along with advanced operations like BGP status or interface monitoring. Instead of using "expect send expect" CLI parsing, we just write readable, maintainable code, and NAPALM handles all the differences for you.

The NAPALM can perform following tasks:

- ***Connect*** to devices over SSH, Telnet, or APIs using a consistent syntax.
- ***Retrieve*** the full running configuration or startup config from any supported device.
- ***Compare*** configurations and spot drift between running and candidate configs, or between device and baseline.
- ***Push*** configuration snippets or full configs, with safe "merge" or "replace" operations.
- ***Rollback*** changes instantly if errors are detected or post-checks fail.
- ***Monitor*** operational data, interface status, ARP/NDP tables, BGP neighbors, LLDP/CDP neighbors, using easy-to-parse Python dictionaries.
- ***Integrate*** with the other automation tools, version control systems, CI/CD pipelines, and alerting.

No matter how many core routers or edge devices we are dealing with, NAPALM gives us efficiency, safety, and repeatability, all in one toolkit.

Setting up NAPALM

We can very easily install the NAPALM and also verify its installation:

```
pip install napalm
import napalm
print(napalm.__version__)
```

After this, we can now use NAPALM in any Python script or Jupyter notebook.

Retrieving & Backing up Device Configurations

Let's go through a typical workflow we would use every day in NCM. We'll start by connecting to devices, then pulling configurations, and finally saving them for version control.

Accessing Device and Config

Let us also imagine that we are managing a Cisco IOS device at **192.168.56.10** with username **admin** and password **yourpassword**. So here, at first, we will create a NAPALM "driver" for IOS and open a connection.

```
from napalm import get_network_driver
driver = get_network_driver('ios')
device = driver('192.168.56.10', 'admin', 'yourpassword')
device.open()
```

If we use the Juniper, Arista, or another platform, then we just have to change the driver string and credentials.

Retrieve Running Config

Next, with the connection live, we can then grab the current running configuration:

```
config = device.get_config()
print(config['running'])
```

This will print the full config as a string and we can also access **config['startup']** or **config['candidate']**.

Save Config for Version Control

After this, we then save to a file, and also timestamped for tracking purpose:

```
from datetime import datetime
```

```
filename =
f"configs/{device.hostname}_running_{datetime.now().strftime('
%Y%m%d_%H%M%S')}.txt"
with open(filename, 'w') as f:
    f.write(config['running'])
```

Now here we must remember to repeat all this for every device in the fleet, and loop through an inventory list and also automate the backups nightly.

Comparing and Validating Configurations

A core feature of NAPALM is the ability to spot "drift", differences between intended (version-controlled) configs and what's running in production. So here, let us consider that we have a gold-standard config in **golden_config.txt** and want to see if our device matches:

```
with open('golden_config.txt', 'r') as f:
    golden = f.read()
device.load_replace_candidate(config=golden)
diffs = device.compare_config()
if diffs:
    print("Config drift detected:")
    print(diffs)
else:
    print("Device matches baseline.")
device.discard_config()
```

This above procees will let us audit compliance, prep for audits, or just ensure every device stays aligned with policy, no surprises during an incident.

Pushing and Rolling Back Configurations

Now, at any point of time, we feel the need to update a device, to which, we simply have to say to roll out a VLAN, change the routing policy, or just to fix a misconfig, so as to make use of the NAPALM's push and rollback flow. The NAPALM allows us to "merge" or "replace" with safety checks before committing.

For example, if we want to push a change:

```
# Load changes (can be a CLI snippet or full config)
```

```
with open('changes.txt', 'r') as f:
    change_snippet = f.read()
device.load_merge_candidate(config=change_snippet)
print(device.compare_config())  # Shows what will change
# If satisfied, commit:
device.commit_config()
# If not, or error found:
# device.discard_config()
```

Now here, if something fails after a push, or we spot an error, we can instantly roll back to the previous config with one command:

```
device.rollback()
```

This is especially valuable in production, where a quick rollback can save minutes or hours of downtime.

Automating NAPALM for Scalability

And to keep track of dozens or hundreds of devices, just store the inventory in a YAML, JSON, or CSV file. It'll loop through the list, connect to each device, and run the backup, compliance, or update logic. We can schedule scripts with cron, launch them from Jenkins, or build them into a full Python web service.

For example, if we want to backup an inventory of devices:

```
import csv
from napalm import get_network_driver
with open('inventory.csv') as f:
    reader = csv.DictReader(f)
    for row in reader:
        driver = get_network_driver(row['driver'])
        device = driver(row['ip'], row['username'],
row['password'])
        device.open()
        config = device.get_config()['running']
```

```
        filename = f"configs/{row['hostname']}_config.txt"
        with open(filename, 'w') as f_out:
            f_out.write(config)
        device.close()
```

The above script will get our config backups automated, versioned, and reproducible. The NAPALM unlocks modern, multi-vendor network configuration management for every engineer, no more device-by-device CLI, no more vendor lock-in, and no more untracked, manual changes.

Automating Configuration Restore Workflows

We can be as disciplined as we want with the configuration management or backup routines, but at some point, we are going to run into a device misconfiguration, firmware crash, or hardware failure. The real test of the network's resilience is not just how well we back up, but how quickly and reliably we can restore service with as little disruption as possible. It's not uncommon for manual recovery to lead to errors, delays, and missed steps, which can result in longer downtime or even incomplete restores.

With ***automating the configuration restore workflows***, we can guarantee that the exact intended version is pushed to each device, that every restore is traceable, and that we can perform recovery confidently under pressure.

Working of Automated Restore Pipeline

A robust restore workflow must be able to connect our version control system, our backup repository, and our device access tool. And such high-assurance pipeline or the workflow is as below:

1. ***Identify*** the failed or misconfigured device, either via monitoring alerts or manual reports.
2. ***Select*** the most recent "known-good" configuration from the Git repository or backup directory.
3. ***Authenticate*** to the target device securely.
4. ***Push*** the configuration, either as a full replacement or a targeted patch, using NAPALM's safe load-and-commit routines.
5. ***Verify*** the restore: check device health, configuration status, and connectivity.
6. ***Log*** every step, timestamp, config version, user ID, device outcome, to an audit trail.
7. ***Alert*** stakeholders of completion, or escalate automatically if the restore fails.

If we colud automate these steps, then it can remove the guesswork and stress during emergencies. And for sure, it will turn the chaos into a predictable, repeatable process.

Building Restore

Now conasidering that most of the backups or all the backups are versioned and stored in a local Git repo, with filenames including device hostname and date. Then in such cases, we can automate the restore as per the following script:

```
from napalm import get_network_driver
import os
def restore_device_config(host, user, pwd, driver,
config_file):
    napalm_driver = get_network_driver(driver)
    device = napalm_driver(host, user, pwd)
    print(f"Connecting to {host}...")
    device.open()
    print(f"Loading config from {config_file}...")
    with open(config_file) as f:
        config_data = f.read()
    device.load_replace_candidate(config=config_data)
    print("Comparing with current config:")
    print(device.compare_config())
    confirm = input("Commit config? (y/n): ").strip().lower()
    if confirm == 'y':
        device.commit_config()
        print("Config restore committed successfully.")
    else:
        device.discard_config()
        print("Restore aborted by user.")
    device.close()
```

Now, in the above script, we:

- Find the correct config (using `git log` or the backup tool).
- Call the script with device info and config path.
- Review the diff before committing.

- Confirm and watch the automated push and audit logging.

In addition to this, we can also batch this for multiple devices, trigger it from a web dashboard, or integrate with the monitoring system for fully hands-off recovery. With a reliable workflow, we turn outages and mistakes from business crises into quick, controlled recoveries, giving the team (and the business) true peace of mind.

Advanced Automation Orchestration

Once our scripts are automating device backups, restores, and configuration pushes, the next challenge is coordination. The orchestration is about managing not just one device, but entire fleets, rolling out changes across data centers, campuses, or hybrid cloud networks in a safe, staged, and policy-driven manner. We move from ad-hoc scripting to predictable, repeatable, and auditable workflows that match the rigor of software engineering. The orchestration also brings automation into the hands of the whole team, including the approvals, notifications, rollback triggers, and compliance checks.

Why Nornir?

The Nornir is a pure Python automation framework for orchestrating tasks across large inventories of devices, giving we inventory management, parallel execution, and pluggable tasks (like NAPALM or Netmiko) in one workflow. Unlike Ansible or Salt, Nornir is code-driven from the start, and integrates naturally with the other Python libraries and automation pipelines.

At first, we quickly install it:

```
pip install nornir nornir-napalm napalm
```

Creating Device Inventory

Next, for orchestration, we have to maintain our network inventory in simple YAML files, as shown below:

- inventory/hosts.yaml

```
router1:
  hostname: 192.168.56.101
  platform: ios
  username: admin
  password: yourpassword
  groups:
```

```
    - routers
router2:
  hostname: 192.168.56.102
  platform: ios
  username: admin
  password: yourpassword
  groups:
    - routers
switch1:
  hostname: 192.168.56.201
  platform: eos
  username: admin
  password: yourpassword
  groups:
    - switches
```

- inventory/groups.yaml

```
routers:
  data:
    role: core
switches:
  data:
    role: access
```

- config.yaml

```
core:
  num_workers: 20
inventory:
  plugin: nornir.plugins.inventory.simple.SimpleInventory
  options:
```

```
    host_file: "inventory/hosts.yaml"
    group_file: "inventory/groups.yaml"
    defaults_file: ""
```

Summary

Throughout this chapter, we explored the core concepts and real-world practices that make modern network configuration management possible and reliable. We understood why precise, auditable, and recoverable configurations are essential for network health, security, and compliance. We learned how leading tools and libraries like NAPALM and Nornir enable us to automate the retrieval, backup, and deployment of configurations across diverse, multi-vendor networks. We practiced how to store every configuration in version control, track changes over time, and restore any device to a known-good state with automated workflows. We saw how configuration restore routines, when automated, can turn high-stress outages into predictable and rapid recoveries.

The chapter walked we through orchestrating multi-device and staged rollouts, implementing validation, approvals, and rollback triggers, and integrating with CI/CD pipelines and event-driven automation. We also reviewed strategies for embedding policy-as-code and compliance checks directly into the automation flows, making configuration management not only repeatable and scalable, but also resilient to mistakes or unexpected changes. By building these skills, we have gained practical, hands-on confidence in keeping the network controlled, auditable, and always ready to recover from any challenge.

CHAPTER 11: ANSIBLE AND PYTHON

Chapter Overview

In this chapter, we will learn how to harness the full potential of Ansible for automating the management of both network and server infrastructure. We will be introduced to the core architecture and workflow of Ansible, discovering how inventories, playbooks, and modules work together to automate complex tasks across dozens or thousands of devices. We will dive deep into creating and executing playbooks that manage everything from user accounts to package installations, configuration files, and ongoing compliance.

Further, the chapter will teach us to leverage variables, loops, and handlers to make the automation dynamic and scalable, and show we how to use roles and includes to organize larger automation projects for long-term success. We will also learn to manage sensitive data securely and see how Ansible and Python can work together for advanced, custom automation scenarios. By the end, we will be able to confidently use Ansible as the backbone for repeatable, auditable, and secure automation in the IT environment, empowering us to respond to change, enforce standards, and eliminate manual error from the daily operations.

Introduction to Ansible

When we look at the evolving world of network automation, one name stands out for its ability to simplify, scale, and standardize operations. And, that is none other than ***Ansible***. Unlike brittle legacy scripts or clunky platform-specific tools, Ansible invites us to automate at any scale using a language that's as close to human-readable as it gets. Its core strength is its declarative approach, we describe the state we want, not every step to achieve it, and Ansible takes care of the details behind the scenes. Whether we manage 10 switches or 10,000 routers, this shift means we focus less on troubleshooting syntax and more on achieving consistent, error-free outcomes.

Control Node, Managed Nodes, and Inventories

The Ansible's design is beautifully simple. Everything starts from a ***control node***, usually the laptop, a jump host, or a shared automation VM. From there, we control a whole fleet of ***managed nodes***: network switches, routers, firewalls, Linux servers, or even cloud VMs. The glue holding everything together is the ***inventory***: a plain text or dynamically generated list of all the managed devices, grouped by function or location. By organizing devices into meaningful groups (**`core_routers`**, **`branch_switches`**, **`dmz_firewalls`**), we make the automation scripts reusable and context-aware. We never have to run dozens of separate scripts, we need to just call a playbook on a group, and Ansible does the rest.

Agentless Automation and Idempotence

A huge part of Ansible's popularity comes from its ***agentless architecture***. Unlike some tools that require us to install special software on every device, the Ansible relies on native protocols, like

SSH for Unix and network devices, or WinRM for Windows. It pushes tiny, purpose-built modules (most written in Python) to the target, executes tasks, then removes them when finished. This means less overhead, fewer moving parts, and fewer ways for automation to "go stale" as environments evolve.

The ***Idempotence*** is another game-changer. When we write an Ansible task to, say, configure a VLAN or update a BGP peer, we can run it again and again without fear, it won't duplicate changes or break what already works. This allows us safely automate even critical production systems and makes Ansible the perfect tool for both one-time projects and ongoing operations.

Playbooks

With Ansible, we don't just automate; we document the network's intended state. Playbooks are written in simple YAML, describing which hosts to target, what variables to use, and what tasks to perform. Anyone, engineer, admin, even a manager who reads YAML, can see exactly what the script will do. This is "infrastructure as code," in a format that's easy to audit, review, or hand off to the next team member. The playbooks can be as simple as configuring a single VLAN, or as sophisticated as orchestrating a full network rollout with multiple stages, approvals, and validations.

Ansible and Python

The synergy between Ansible and Python is unmatched. Not only are Ansible's own modules built in Python (making it easy to extend or customize), but we can seamlessly blend Ansible playbooks into larger Python automation flows. We can call Ansible from a Python script, pass variables or inventory dynamically, or trigger playbooks based on logic, monitoring alerts, or external events. On the flip side, we can embed custom Python code into playbooks via filters, plugins, or lookup scripts, adding dynamic calculations, inventory logic, or validation that goes far beyond static YAML. This makes Ansible not just a tool, but a bridge between human-readable automation and Python-powered logic for even the most complex workflows.

Human-Centric and Scalable

Because everything is defined in plain text, reviewed and versioned in Git, and tested before rollout, Ansible playbooks become the living documentation and the rapid recovery plan. If a device needs to be rebuilt or replaced, just rerun the playbook, no scrambling for hand-written notes or ancient backups. The playbooks are also easy to share, extend, and adapt as teams grow or requirements change.

The leap from hand-crafted scripts or manual CLI to Ansible-driven automation is often the biggest force multiplier a network engineer can experience. Suddenly, we can safely make changes across hundreds of devices, enforce standards, and recover from outages with a single command. The playbooks can be chained together, triggered by monitoring events, or integrated with chatops so anyone (with permission) can deploy or repair the network.

Setting up Ansible on Windows

The Windows Subsystem for Linux (WSL) allows us to run a genuine Linux distribution, like Ubuntu, directly inside the Windows 10 or 11 system, sharing the local drives and files. This means we get full access to Ansible and other open-source tools in a familiar command line, with almost zero performance penalty. And there's no need for dual-boot or heavyweight virtualization.

Setting up WSL

We can start the installation, beginning with PowerShell ***as Administrator*** and running the following:

```
wsl --install
```

This installs WSL 2 and downloads Ubuntu by default. If we already have WSL 1, upgrade with:

```
wsl --update
```

After the reboot, we then launch the "Ubuntu" app from the Start Menu. The first launch prompts us to create a Linux username and password.

Next, inside our new Linux shell, we then type:

```
sudo apt update && sudo apt upgrade
sudo apt install python3 python3-pip python3-venv sshpass
```

This ensures Python, Pip, and SSH support are ready. After this, we then install Ansible:

```
sudo apt-add-repository --yes --update ppa:ansible/ansible
sudo apt install ansible
ansible --version
```

We should see the current version and details. We can now create inventories, playbooks, and use Ansible modules just as on any Linux server. Now the Windows C: drive is accessible at **`/mnt/c/`**. And then we can edit playbooks with VS Code in Windows, then run them from the Linux shell.

Using Linux VM on Windows

If we prefer to use a dedicated virtual machine (VM), then there are various tools available like ***VirtualBox*** or ***VMware Workstation Player*** that let us run a full Linux system. The process is very simple as follows:

- Download an Ubuntu ISO and create a VM.
- Follow the same steps (update, install Python and Ansible).
- Share folders or use SSH for file access.

This whole process is often used in enterprise environments where WSL may be restricted.

With this setup, we are able to run the real Ansible, with no emulation, and with no compatibility headaches, and definitely no vendor lock-in. Everything we learn about Ansible on Linux will apply perfectly, so we are ready to automate networks, servers, or cloud from any Windows workstation.

Ansible Modules, Tasks and Playbooks

The ***Modules*** are the building blocks of Ansible. They are small, self-contained programs (usually written in Python) that perform discrete functions: creating a user, copying a file, configuring an interface, or managing a service. When we "run Ansible," we are really running a series of modules against one or more hosts. The ***Tasks*** are the steps inside the playbook. Each task calls a module, passing parameters that tell Ansible what we want to do. Think of a task as a single instruction, like "ensure nginx is installed," or "set hostname to 'core-router-1'." And the ***Playbooks*** are YAML files that organize tasks into plays and apply them to groups of hosts from the inventory. Playbooks let us orchestrate complex automation: running tasks in sequence, with variables, handlers, logic, and error handling, all in a human-readable format.

Writing First Playbook

Let us try to configure a group of Linux hosts, ensuring **`nginx`** is installed and started, and a welcome page is deployed. Our playbook should be looking something like the following:

```
---
- name: Configure web servers
  hosts: webservers
  become: yes
  tasks:
    - name: Install nginx
      apt:
        name: nginx
        state: present
    - name: Ensure nginx is running
```

```
    service:
      name: nginx
      state: started
      enabled: yes
  - name: Deploy welcome page
    copy:
      src: files/index.html
      dest: /var/www/html/index.html
      owner: www-data
      group: www-data
      mode: '0644'
```

After this, save this as **web_setup.yml** and run:

```
ansible-playbook -i inventory.txt web_setup.yml
```

The output should be something like this:

```
TASK [Install nginx] ***
ok: [10.10.10.101]
ok: [10.10.10.102]
TASK [Ensure nginx is running] ***
changed: [10.10.10.101]
changed: [10.10.10.102]
TASK [Deploy welcome page] ***
changed: [10.10.10.101]
changed: [10.10.10.102]
```

This Ansible's output tells us whether each task was "ok" (already done), "changed" (applied), or "failed" (error).

Making Playbooks Dynamic

The variables make the playbooks powerful and reusable. We can define them in inventories, playbooks, extra-vars, or external files.

```
vars:
  web_content: "Hello, {{ inventory_hostname }}!"
tasks:
  - name: Deploy dynamic welcome page
    copy:
      content: "{{ web_content }}"
      dest: /var/www/html/index.html
```

We can also use ***facts***, data gathered by Ansible about each host (IP, OS, memory, etc.), to make decisions dynamically.

```
tasks:
  - name: Print OS version
    debug:
      msg: "This server runs {{ ansible_distribution }} {{
ansible_distribution_version }}"
```

Conditionals and Loops

Now here, what if we want to run tasks only on some hosts or under certain conditions? In such situations, we can try to make use of the **`when`** clauses.

```
tasks:
  - name: Reboot Debian hosts
    reboot:
    when: ansible_distribution == "Debian"
```

There are loops that let us to repeat a task with different items.

```
tasks:
  - name: Add multiple users
    user:
      name: "{{ item }}"
      state: present
```

```
    loop:
      - alice
      - bob
      - carol
```

Handlers

The handlers are special tasks triggered by **notify** when another task changes something. Let me show we how to use the handlers for restarts or reloads in the following script:

```
tasks:
  - name: Update config
    template:
      src: nginx.conf.j2
      dest: /etc/nginx/nginx.conf
    notify: Reload nginx
handlers:
  - name: Reload nginx
    service:
      name: nginx
      state: reloaded
```

If the config changes, nginx is reloaded once at the end.

Includes and Roles

With time the playbooks are going to grow. We may need to break them up for reuse and clarity. So here, we can use **include_tasks**, **import_tasks**, or organize into ***roles***.

Following is the sample directory layout:

```
site.yml
roles/
  web/
    tasks/
```

```
    main.yml
  files/
    index.html
  templates/
    nginx.conf.j2
  handlers/
    main.yml
```

In the playbook:

```
- hosts: webservers
  roles:
    - web
```

Here, the roles make projects modular, shareable and maintainable.

Error Handling and Idempotence

The Ansible is designed for ***idempotence***. Even if we run the playbook multiple times, it yields the same result. But there could be some situations when it could fail. So, in such situations, we can use **`ignore_errors: yes`**, to keep going. Or we can use **`block`** and **`rescue`**/**`always`** to handle if we thing the error recovery is going to be complex.

```
tasks:
  - block:
      - name: Try risky thing
        command: /usr/bin/risky
    rescue:
      - name: Fallback if risky fails
        debug:
          msg: "Risky operation failed, running fallback."
```

Writing Custom Modules

For device or logic not covered by built-in modules, we can write our own in Python. The custom modules receive arguments as JSON, perform actions, and return results as JSON. See the following sample program. Here, we can name the file as ***my_echo.py***:

```
#!/usr/bin/python
from ansible.module_utils.basic import AnsibleModule
def main():
    module = AnsibleModule(
        argument_spec=dict(msg=dict(type='str',
required=True))
    )
    result = dict(changed=False, echo=module.params['msg'])
    module.exit_json(**result)
if __name__ == '__main__':
    main()
```

After this, we simply call this from our playbook as a local module.

Sample Program: Pushing VLANs

We now try to learn through a easy simple program in which we try to automate the VLAN deployment on Cisco IOS devices.

Following is we create a vlan.yml file within our playbook:

```
- name: Push VLANs to switches
  hosts: switches
  gather_facts: no
  vars:
    vlans:
      - id: 10
        name: USERS
      - id: 20
        name: GUEST
  tasks:
    - name: Ensure VLANs present
```

```
      ios_config:
        lines:
          - "vlan {{ item.id }}"
          - "name {{ item.name }}"
      loop: "{{ vlans }}"
```

Given below is an inventory example:

```
[switches]
192.168.56.201
192.168.56.202
```

We then run:

```
ansible-playbook -i inventory.txt playbooks/vlan.yml
```

The following is the expected output:

```
TASK [Ensure VLANs present] ***
changed: [192.168.56.201] => (item={'id': 10, 'name':
'USERS'})
changed: [192.168.56.201] => (item={'id': 20, 'name':
'GUEST'})
changed: [192.168.56.202] => (item={'id': 10, 'name':
'USERS'})
changed: [192.168.56.202] => (item={'id': 20, 'name':
'GUEST'})
```

With this, all the targeted switches now have VLAN 10 and VLAN 20 configured, safely, idempotently, and with clear tracking.

Playbook to Configure Servers

It is highly common about when we make use of Ansible to configure servers, our playbook becomes the "single source of truth" for server state, whether we are onboarding a new Linux host, hardening security, or preparing application dependencies. The playbooks can manage everything, including the package installs, service enablement, user setup, firewall rules, storage, and custom configuration files.

We will see all this in the following subtopics:

Defining Inventory and Groups

For example, let us think of a situation wherein we want to manage both, Ubuntu and CentOS servers across different roles. So, in such a situation, we create an inventory (**inventory.ini**) as below:

```
[ubuntu_web]
10.10.10.101 ansible_user=ubuntu
[centos_db]
10.10.10.201 ansible_user=centos
[all_servers:children]
ubuntu_web
centos_db
```

This allows us target hosts by OS or function, using groups for modularity.

Writing Role-based Playbook

Now here, we will configure all the servers to:

- Ensure a user "deploy" exists
- Update all packages
- Install and configure **nginx** (on Ubuntu) or **httpd** (on CentOS)
- Harden SSH
- Deploy an application config from a template

So here, we will create the **playbooks/server_setup.yml** and all th above outlined objectives will be scripted in the below program:

```
---
- name: Configure all servers for application deployment
  hosts: all_servers
  become: yes
  vars_files:
    - vars/global.yml
  tasks:
```

```yaml
  - name: Ensure deploy user exists
    user:
      name: deploy
      state: present
      groups: sudo
  - name: Update all packages (Ubuntu)
    apt:
      update_cache: yes
      upgrade: dist
    when: ansible_os_family == "Debian"
  - name: Update all packages (CentOS)
    yum:
      name: "*"
      state: latest
    when: ansible_os_family == "RedHat"
  - name: Install and configure nginx (Ubuntu)
    apt:
      name: nginx
      state: present
    when: ansible_os_family == "Debian"
  - name: Install and configure httpd (CentOS)
    yum:
      name: httpd
      state: present
    when: ansible_os_family == "RedHat"
  - name: Harden SSH
    lineinfile:
      path: /etc/ssh/sshd_config
      regexp: '^PasswordAuthentication'
```

```
        line: 'PasswordAuthentication no'
      notify: Restart SSH
    - name: Deploy application config
      template:
        src: app_config.j2
        dest: /etc/myapp/config.yml
        owner: deploy
        group: deploy
        mode: '0640'
  handlers:
    - name: Restart SSH
      service:
        name: ssh
        state: restarted
      when: ansible_os_family == "Debian"
    - name: Restart SSH (CentOS)
      service:
        name: sshd
        state: restarted
      when: ansible_os_family == "RedHat"
```

Variable Files and Template Management

There will be a file called **vars/global.yml** which might hold environment-wide variables (like usernames, default passwords, or app ports):

```
app_port: 8080
deploy_user: deploy
```

We can make use of a template like **app_config.j2** that let us inject the above variables into config files dynamically:

```
server:
```

```
  port: {{ app_port }}
  user: {{ deploy_user }}
```

Executing Playbook

Next, we will then run the playbook from our Ansible control node:

```
ansible-playbook -i inventory.ini playbooks/server_setup.yml
```

With this, we will see a step-by-step log, showing which tasks ran, which were skipped (based on **`when`** conditions), and any changes made.

For the easy understanding, I have described how the output would be:

```
TASK [Ensure deploy user exists] ***
changed: [10.10.10.101]
changed: [10.10.10.201]
TASK [Update all packages (Ubuntu)] ***
ok: [10.10.10.101]
skipping: [10.10.10.201]
TASK [Update all packages (CentOS)] ***
skipping: [10.10.10.101]
changed: [10.10.10.201]
...
```

Securing Sensitive Data

In situation or primarily for production, we will be wanting to encrypt the secrets (passwords, API tokens) using ***Ansible Vault***:

```
ansible-vault create vars/secrets.yml
```

And then we need to just reference those in our playbook. This will keep thes ensitive data out of source control.

This whole approach means any server, new or existing, can be brought into a compliant, ready state with a single command. We can rebuild, audit, or extend the setup instantly. Playbooks become the runbook, documentation, and rapid recovery tool. If the application or security standards change, update the playbook and rerun, every host converges to the intent.

Ansible for Managing Softwares

With even handful of servers, keeping the track of which applications are installed, their versions, and their running states is a major challenge. Imagine if we multiply this by tens, hundreds, or thousands of hosts, the manual management becomes impossible. The power of Ansible solves this with its declarative, repeatable playbooks. We specify ***what state we want***, which software should be installed, which version, which should be absent, and which services should always be running, and Ansible converges every server to match, every time we run the playbook.

Package Management

Let us take a situation wherein we are required to ensure **`nginx`** and **`git`** are present on all web servers, and that **`telnet`** is explicitly removed (for security compliance). So, for this, we can write:

```
- name: Manage server software
  hosts: webservers
  become: yes
  tasks:
    - name: Install essential software
      apt:
        name: ['nginx', 'git']
        state: present
      when: ansible_os_family == 'Debian'
    - name: Install essential software (RedHat)
      yum:
        name:
          - nginx
          - git
        state: present
      when: ansible_os_family == 'RedHat'
    - name: Remove insecure software
      apt:
        name: telnet
```

```
        state: absent
      when: ansible_os_family == 'Debian'
    - name: Remove insecure software (RedHat)
      yum:
        name: telnet
        state: absent
      when: ansible_os_family == 'RedHat'
```

This allows us enforce organization-wide standards, eliminate risky software, and keep environments consistent with a single command.

Managing Post-Install Service State

When we install software, we only half the work. We also got to make sure the services are running and set to start on boot.

So here, we will make use of Ansible's idempotence capability as below:

```
tasks:
    - name: Ensure nginx is started and enabled (Debian)
      service:
        name: nginx
        state: started
        enabled: yes
      when: ansible_os_family == 'Debian'
    - name: Ensure nginx is started and enabled (RedHat)
      service:
        name: nginx
        state: started
        enabled: yes
      when: ansible_os_family == 'RedHat'
```

In the above program, if the service is already running, nothing changes; if it's down, it's started automatically.

Handling Software Upgrades

And if we need to enforce a specific version or upgrade an app, we've got we covered. We can specify the version we want in the playbook.

```
- name: Ensure specific version of git is installed
  apt:
    name: git=1:2.25.1-1ubuntu3.10
    state: present
  when: ansible_os_family == 'Debian'
```

Or, we can simply upgrade all packages to the latest:

```
- name: Upgrade all packages (Debian)
  apt:
    upgrade: dist
    update_cache: yes
  when: ansible_os_family == 'Debian'
```

Working with Third-Party and Custom Software

There are challenges or business demand wherein we have to manage tools outside the main repositories (for example, Docker or a proprietary app). In such cases, we can make use of the **get_url**, **unarchive**, or **pip** modules for custom installs:

```
- name: Download custom app
  get_url:
    url: https://example.com/releases/myapp.tar.gz
    dest: /tmp/myapp.tar.gz
 - name: Extract app
  unarchive:
    src: /tmp/myapp.tar.gz
    dest: /opt/myapp
    remote_src: yes
```

Or we can use **pip** for Python packages:

```
- name: Install Python package (requests)
  pip:
    name: requests
    state: present
```

Auditing and Enforcing Software Compliance

And if we have to ensure that only the approved software is present, then in such scenarios we can use the Ansible's **package_facts** module to run audit on the packages:

```
- name: Gather installed packages
  package_facts:
  when: ansible_os_family == 'Debian'
 - name: List forbidden packages
  debug:
    var: ansible_facts.packages['telnet']
  when: "'telnet' in ansible_facts.packages"
```

We can also loop over a list of forbidden packages and ensure they are absent:

```
vars:
   forbidden_software:
     - telnet
     - ftp
 tasks:
   - name: Remove forbidden packages
     apt:
       name: "{{ item }}"
       state: absent
     loop: "{{ forbidden_software }}"
     when: ansible_os_family == 'Debian'
```

In addition, if we ever feel that our software management logic becomes too complex for YAML, we can then call the Python scripts using **script** or **command** module, or create custom Ansible modules in Python which can then perform and carry out the advanced checks, dynamic version fetching, and reporting on behalf of us.

Sample Program: Enforcing Application Stack

Here's a hypothetical situation, where we want every app server to have nginx, gunicorn, and a custom Python app installed, with all services running and up-to-date. For such a case, we create a following playbook that might work for all such needs:

```
- name: Enforce app stack on all servers
  hosts: app_servers
  become: yes
  vars:
    python_packages:
      - gunicorn
      - flask
  tasks:
    - name: Ensure nginx is installed
      apt:
        name: nginx
        state: present
      when: ansible_os_family == 'Debian'
    - name: Install required Python packages
      pip:
        name: "{{ python_packages }}"
        state: present
    - name: Deploy custom app code
      git:
        repo: 'https://github.com/org/app.git'
        dest: /srv/app
    - name: Configure and start gunicorn
```

```
    systemd:
      name: gunicorn
      state: started
      enabled: yes
```

This above is a playbook that can run, audit, re-run, and enforce all such standards fleet-wide. Instead of firefighting servers one by one, the playbooks become the "contract" for how every machine is built, what it runs, and how it stays secure and up to date. Software sprawl, drift, and shadow IT are minimized. When someone asks, "What's on this server?" or "Why is telnet still installed?", the answer is always in the playbook, not someone's memory.

Summary

Throughout this chapter, we gained a real-world, hands-on understanding of how Ansible streamlines and scales IT automation for both network and server management. We learned the underlying principles that make Ansible so effective, including its agentless architecture, idempotent task execution, and human-readable YAML playbooks that double as living documentation. We explored the power of organizing devices and servers in structured inventories, then saw how playbooks and tasks can automate everything from user creation and software installation to service management and configuration enforcement.

We practiced handling complex scenarios using variables, loops, handlers, conditionals, and error management, and discovered how Ansible roles promote modular, reusable code for larger projects. We saw practical examples of managing both Linux and Windows hosts, handling software versioning, auditing compliance, and securely managing sensitive data with Ansible Vault. By the end of this chapter, we also understood how to combine Ansible automation with Python for custom workflows, integrating audit, orchestration, and reporting into the infrastructure as code journey. This chapter has equipped us to deploy, secure, and maintain IT environments of any size, confidently and repeatedly.

Index

A

access control 6, 7, 9, 70, 83, 98
ACL 83
aiohttp 89, 90
Ansible modules 123, 139
Ansible playbooks 122
ARP 8, 55, 57, 69, 97, 111
asynchronous programming 86, 87, 92
asyncio 86, 87, 88, 89, 90, 91, 92, 93
automation pipelines 91, 117

B

BGP 8, 83, 111, 122
bridges 83

C

capacity testing 103
change management 79, 97, 99
concurrency 88, 89, 90, 92
configuration drift 43, 83
configuration files 121, 130
configuration management 9, 10, 108, 115, 119
core routers 111
coroutines 86, 88, 89, 93

D

data structures 5
device onboarding 83, 87
DHCP 8, 83
dictionaries 5, 10, 46, 111
DNS . 8, 9, 27, 28, 34, 35, 36, 37, 38, 69, 70, 76, 97, 101

E

encryption 8, 27, 55, 66, 68, 70, 74
error handling 2, 10, 22, 25, 31, 38, 91, 92, 93, 111, 124
event loop 86, 88, 89, 93
event-driven 9, 76, 83, 84, 87, 89, 92, 108, 119
exceptions 29, 81, 100

F

firewall rules 13, 38, 67, 69, 83, 97, 130
firewalls 7, 9, 10, 23, 35, 54, 66, 67, 70, 74, 78, 83, 96, 98, 108, 111, 121
FTP 16, 27, 28, 30, 31, 34, 38, 69
functions 2, 6, 7, 10, 16, 88, 124

H

HTTPS 8, 27, 28, 30, 38, 69
httpx 2, 4, 5, 8
hybrid networks 83

I

ICMP 62, 69, 70, 98, 99, 100
idempotence 128, 136
idempotent 44
intrusion detection 9, 66, 74
iperf3 54, 62, 63, 64, 95, 96, 98, 99, 100, 106
IPv4 8, 14
IPv6 8

L

latency testing 64
list comprehensions 6
lists 5, 6, 10, 98
load testing 98
locust 101, 102, 103
log analysis 10
logging 6, 10, 30, 34, 40, 48, 82, 93, 97, 98, 102, 117

M

modules 2, 6, 10, 28, 34, 68, 121, 122, 124, 128, 137
MPLS 8

N

napalm 2, 110, 112, 114, 116, 117
NAT 25
netmiko 2, 42, 44, 46, 50, 79
network configuration 108, 115, 119
network monitoring 9, 54, 64, 99
network simulation 96, 104
Network Topologies 7

O

operators 6, 10

orchestration.......... 8, 76, 84, 108, 117
OSPF.......... 8

P

packet inspection.......... 7
paramiko.......... 2, 42, 51, 71
penetration testing.......... 96, 99
performance analysis.......... 63
performance testing.......... 64
ping.......... 62, 63, 64, 73, 88, 96, 97, 99, 100
ping3.......... 54, 62, 64, 95, 96, 99, 106
pip..... 3, 4, 5, 29, 35, 42, 56, 61, 62, 69, 90, 91, 99, 100, 101, 104, 110, 112, 117, 123, 137, 138
pysnmp.......... 2, 8, 56, 57, 58, 59, 60

R

real-time monitoring.......... 20
reliability testing.......... 96, 102, 103
requests8, 27, 28, 29, 30, 33, 38, 69, 76, 77, 78, 79, 80, 81, 82, 83, 84, 87, 88, 90, 92, 93, 99, 102, 138
routers 2, 7, 8, 9, 10, 30, 40, 54, 55, 56, 76, 78, 83, 104, 105, 108, 111, 118, 121

S

scapy.......... 2, 61, 69, 70
scheduled tasks.......... 10
security compliance.......... 135
service enablement.......... 130
simpy.......... 104, 105, 106
SMTP.......... 16, 28, 32, 38, 77
SNMP... 2, 8, 9, 40, 54, 55, 56, 57, 58, 59, 60, 61, 63, 64, 69, 83, 98
socket library.......... 12, 14, 16, 25, 28, 34
software updates.......... 67
SSH..... 2, 8, 9, 16, 41, 42, 43, 45, 52, 66, 67, 89, 92, 111, 122, 123, 124, 131, 132, 133
SSL.......... 9, 28, 33, 66, 68, 70, 74
stress testing.......... 98
string formatting.......... 10
strings.......... 6, 20
subprocess.......... 71, 73
switches..... 2, 7, 9, 43, 54, 55, 56, 76, 78, 83, 89, 90, 96, 104, 108, 111, 118, 121, 129, 130
systemctl restart.......... 72

T

task scheduling.......... 93
TCP.... 8, 9, 11, 12, 13, 14, 16, 17, 18, 19, 20, 21, 22, 25, 28, 66, 70, 97, 98
telnet.......... 17, 18, 20, 135, 136, 138, 140
troubleshooting. 2, 8, 10, 12, 13, 27, 34, 35, 38, 60, 74, 82, 121
type hints.......... 6, 10

U

UDP.... 8, 9, 11, 12, 13, 14, 15, 16, 20, 21, 22, 23, 24, 25, 38, 70, 97, 98, 101
user management.......... 72

V

variables.......... 2, 6, 10, 55, 121, 122, 124, 125, 133
virtual environment.......... 10, 104
VLAN....... 8, 9, 40, 43, 44, 45, 49, 76, 80, 113, 122, 129, 130
VPN.......... 66, 70, 72, 73

Epilogue

As we finish up this second edition of Python Networking 101, I want to reflect on your journey through these chapters. You started with the building blocks of Python and networking, and step by step, you turned that knowledge into actionable skills. You moved from writing simple socket programs to interacting with real-world protocols, automating configurations, securing networks, and orchestrating infrastructures at scale. You've worked with some pretty sophisticated tools like Netmiko, Paramiko, NAPALM, AsyncIO, SNMP, Locust, SimPy, and Ansible, but they were all pretty straightforward and useful in the real world. The idea behind every example, code block, and concept was to help you build your confidence, layer by layer. You've seen how Python can control devices, test performance, analyze data, secure communication, and automate repetitive workflows. Even better, you've seen how combining scripting with networking principles opens up new possibilities that go way beyond manual administration. The real skill you need as a modern network professional comes when you can go from understanding a protocol to automating its configuration or testing its performance.

This book wasn't about memorizing commands or chasing complex edge cases. It was about giving you the clarity and hands-on practice to take control of networks through code. No matter what you decide to focus on—automation, security, testing, or orchestration—the skills you've gained here are going to be a huge asset in the real world. The libraries and methods you've learned will keep changing, but your ability to approach a problem, break it down, and solve it programmatically will stay a lasting skill. I hope you've enjoyed this journey as much as I enjoyed building it, and you'll decide what to do next.

Take these skills, apply them boldly, and keep pushing the boundaries of what you can automate and create.

Thank You

www.ingramcontent.com/pod-product-compliance
Lightning Source LLC
Chambersburg PA
CBHW080215170726
48282CB00030B/1132
* 9 7 8 8 1 9 7 4 1 6 5 0 7 *